Clara E. C. Waters

Angels in Art

Clara E. C. Waters

Angels in Art

ISBN/EAN: 9783337300470

Printed in Europe, USA, Canada, Australia, Japan

Cover: Foto ©Thomas Meinert / pixelio.de

More available books at **www.hansebooks.com**

ANGELS IN ART

BY

CLARA ERSKINE CLEMENT

AUTHOR OF
"A HANDBOOK OF LEGENDARY ART,"
"PAINTERS, SCULPTORS, ARCHITECTS, AND ENGRAVERS,"
"ARTISTS OF THE NINETEENTH CENTURY,"
ETC.

Illustrated

BOSTON
L. C. PAGE AND COMPANY
(INCORPORATED)
1898

CONTENTS.

ILLUSTRATIONS.

———◆———

ANGELS IN ART.

CHAPTER I.

INTRODUCTORY.

NGELS and archangels, cherubim and seraphim, and all the
glorious hosts of heaven were
a fruitful source of inspiration to the oldest painters and sculptors whose works
are known to us, while the artists of our
more practical, less dreamful age are, from
time to time, inspired to reproduce their
conceptions of the guardian angels of
our race.

The Almighty declared to Job that the
creation of the world was welcomed with
shouts of joy by "all the sons of God,"

and the story of the words and works of
the angels written in the Scriptures —
from the placing of the cherubim at the
east of the Garden of Eden, to the worship of the angel by John, in the last
chapter of Revelation — presents them to
us as heavenly guides, consolers, protect-
ors, and reprovers of human beings.

What study is more charming and rest-
ful than that of the angels as set forth in
Holy Writ and the writings of the early
Church? or more interesting to observe
than the manner in which the artists of
various nations and periods have expressed
their ideas concerning these celestial messengers of God?   What more fascinating,
more stimulating to the imagination and
further removed from the exhausting ten-
sion of our day and generation?

The Old Testament represents the angels as an innumerable host, discerning
good and evil by reason of superior intel-

ligence, and without passion doing the will of God. Having the power to slay, it is only exercised by the command of the Almighty, and not until after the Captivity do we read of evil angels who work wickedness among men. In fact, after this time the Hebrews seem to have added much to their angelic theory and faith which harmonizes with the religion of the Chaldeans, and with the teaching of Zoroaster.

The angels of the New Testament, while exempt from need and suffering, have sympathy with human sorrow, rejoice over repentance of sin, attend on prayerful souls, and conduct the spirits of the just to heaven when the earthly life is ended.

One may doubt, however, if from the Scriptural teaching concerning angels would emanate the universal interest in their representation, and the personal

sympathy with it, which is commonly
shared by all sorts and conditions of men,
did they not cherish a belief—consciously
or otherwise—that beings superior to
themselves exist, and employ their superhuman powers for the blessing of our
race, and for the welfare of individuals.
Evidently Spenser felt this when he wrote:

" How oft do they their silver bowers leave,
And come to succor us that succor want ?
How oft do they with golden pinions cleave
The flitting skies, like flying pursuivant,
Against foul fiends, to aid us militant ?
They for us fight, they watch, and duly ward,
And their bright squadrons round about us plant,
And all for love, and nothing for reward !
Oh, why should heavenly God to men have such re-
    gard ! "

As early as the fourth century the
Christian Church had developed a pro-
found belief in the existence of both
good and evil angels,—" the foul fiends "
and " bright squadrons " of Spenser's lines,

—the former ever tempting human beings to sin, and the indulgence of their
lower natures; the latter inciting them to
pursue good, forsaking evil and pressing
forward to the perfect Christian life. This
faith is devoutly maintained in the writings of the Fathers of the Church, in
which we are also taught that angelic
aid may be invoked in our need, and
that a consciousness of the abiding
presence of celestial beings should be
a supreme solace to human sorrow and
suffering.

It remained for the theologians of the
Middle Ages to exercise their fruitful
imaginations in originating a systematic
classification of the Orders of the Heavenly Host, and assigning to each rank
its distinctive office. The warrant for
these discriminations may seem insufficient to sceptical minds, but as their
results are especially manifest in the

works of the old masters, some knowledge of them is necessary to the student of Art; without it a large proportion of the famous religious pictures of the world are utterly void of meaning.

Speaking broadly, this classification was based on that of St. Paul, when he speaks of " the principalities and powers in heavenly places," and of " thrones and dominions ; " on the account by Jude of the fall of the " angels which kept not their first estate;" on the triumphs of the Archangel Michael, and a few other texts of Scripture. Upon these premises the angelic host was divided into three hierarchies, and these again into nine choirs.

The first hierarchy embraces seraphim, cherubim, and thrones, the first mention being sometimes given to the cherubim. Dionysius the Areopagite — to whom St. Paul confided all that he had seen, when transported to the seventh heaven — ac-

cords the first rank to the seraphim,
while the familiar hymn of St. Ambrose
has accustomed us to saying, "To Thee,
cherubim and seraphim continually do
cry." Dante gives preference to Dionysius as an authority, and says of him:

> "For he had learn'd
> Both this and much beside of these our orbs
> From an eye-witness to Heaven's mysteries."

The second hierarchy includes the
dominations, virtues, and powers; the
third, princedoms, archangels, and angels. The first hierarchy receives its
glory directly from the Almighty, and
transmits it to the second, which, in
turn, illuminates the third, which is especially dedicated to the care and service
of the human race.

From the third hierarchy come the
ministers and messengers of God; the
second is composed of governors, and
the first of councillors. The choristers

of heaven are also angels, and the making of music is an important angelic duty.

The seraphim immediately surround
the throne of God, and are ever lost in
adoration and love, which is expressed
in their very name, seraph coming from
a Hebrew root, meaning love. The cherubim also worship the Creator, and are
assigned to some special duties; they
are superior in knowledge, and the word
cherub, also from the Hebrew, signifies
to know. Thrones sustain the seat of the
Almighty.

The second hierarchy governs the elements and the stars. Princedoms protect
earthly monarchies, while archangels and
angels are the agents of God in his deal-
ings with humanity. The title of angel,
signifying a messenger, may be, and is,
given to a man bearing important tidings.
Thus the Evangelists are represented with
wings, and John the Baptist is, in this

sense, an angel. The Greeks sometimes represent Christ with wings, and call him " The Great Angel of the Will of God."

Very early in the history of Art a system of religious symbolism existed, a knowledge of which greatly enhances the pleasure derived from representations of sacred subjects. In no case was this symbolism more carefully observed than in the representations of angels. The aureole or nimbus is never omitted from the head of an angel, and is always, wherever used, the symbol of sanctity.

Wings are the distinctive angelic symbol, and are emblematic of spirit, power, and swiftness. Seraphim and cherubim are usually represented by heads with one, two, or three pairs of wings, which symbolize pure spirit, informed by love and intelligence; the head is an emblem of the soul, the love, the knowledge, while the wings have their usual significance.

This manner of representing the two highest orders of angels is very ancient, and in the earliest instances in existence the faces are human, thoughtful, and mature. Gradually they became child-like, and were intended to express innocence, and later they degenerated into absurd little baby heads, with little wings folded under the chin. These in no sense convey the original, spiritual significance of the seraphic and cherubic head.

The first Scriptural mention of cherubim with wings occurs after the departure of the Israelites from Egypt, Exodus xxv., 20: "And the cherubim shall stretch forth their wings on high, covering the mercy seat." Isaiah gives warrant for six wings, as frequently represented in Art, and so vividly described by Milton:

"A seraph winged; six wings he wore to shade
His lineaments divine; the pair that clad
Each shoulder broad, came mantling o'er his breast

PERUGINO. — A SIX-WINGED CHERUB. (FROM THE AS-
SUMPTION OF THE VIRGIN.

With regal ornament; the middle pair
Girt like a starry zone his waist, and round   .
Skirted his loins and thighs with downy gold
And colors dipp'd in heaven; the third, his feet
Shadow'd from either heel with feather'd mail,
Sky-tinctured grain."

In Ezekiel we read that "their wings
were stretched upward when they flew;
when they stood they let down their
wings." There is, no doubt, Scriptural
authority for representing angels' wings
in the most realistic manner, since Daniel
says "they had wings like a fowl." Is it
not more desirable, however, to see angel-
wings rather than bird-wings? The more
devout and imaginative artists succeeded
in overcoming the commonplace in this
regard by various devices. For example,
Orcagna, in the Campo Santo at Pisa,
makes the bodies of his angels to end
in delicate wings instead of legs; in some
old pictures the wings fade into a cloudy
vapor, or burst into flames. In one of

Raphael's frescoes in the Vatican, we see fiery cherubs, their hair, wings, and limbs ending in glowing flames, while their faces are full of spirit and intelligence. Certainly, if anywhere purely impressionist painting is acceptable and fitting, it is in the portrayal of heavenly wings.

Mrs. Jameson, in writing of this subject, says, " Infinitely more beautiful and consistent are the nondescript wings which the early painters gave their angels: large, — so large that, when the glorious creature is represented as at rest, they droop from the shoulders to the ground; with long, slender feathers, eyed sometimes like the peacock's·train, bedropped with gold like the pheasant's breast, tinted with azure and violet and crimson, ' Colors dipp'd in Heaven,' — they are really angel-wings, not bird-wings."

It is interesting to note that wings were used by the artists of ancient

Egypt, Babylon, Nineveh, and Etruria as symbols of might, majesty, and divine beauty.

The representation of great numbers of angels, surrounding the Deity, the Trinity, or the glorified Virgin, is known as a Glory of Angels, and is most expressive and poetical when æsthetically portrayed. A Glory, when properly represented, is composed of the hierarchies of angels in circles, each hierarchy in its proper order. Complete Glories, with nine circles, are exceedingly rare. Many artists contented themselves with two or three, and sometimes but a single circle, thus symbolizing the symbol of the Glory.

The nine choirs of angels are represented in various ways when not in a Glory, and are frequently seen in ancient frescoes, mosaics, and sculptures. Sometimes each choir has three figures, thus symbolizing the Trinity; again, two figures stand for each choir, and occasionally nine figures personate the three hierarchies; in the last representation careful attention was given to colors as well as to symbols.

The Princedoms and Powers of Heaven are represented by rows and groups of angels, all wearing the same dress and the same tiara, and bearing the orb of sovereignty and wands like sceptres.

One of the most important elements in the proper painting of seraphs and cherubs was the use of color, while greater freedom was permitted in the portrayal of other angelic orders. In a Glory, for example, the inner circle should be glowing red, the symbol of love; the second, blue, the emblem of light, which again symbolizes knowledge.

Angelic symbolism in its purity makes the " blue-eyed seraphim " and the " smiling cherubim " equally incorrect, since the seraph should be glowing with divine love, and the face of the cherub should be expressive of serious meditation, — as Milton says, "the Cherub Contemplation." The familiar cherubim beneath Raphael's famous Madonna di San Sisto, in the Dresden Gallery, are exquisite illustrations of this thoughtfulness.

The colors of the oldest pictures, of the illuminated manuscripts, the stained glass, and the painted sculptures were most carefully considered. Gradually, however, the color law was less faithfully observed, until, at the end of the fifteenth and the beginning of the sixteenth centuries, it was not unusual to see the wings of cherubim in various colors, while cherub heads were represented as floating in clouds with no apparent wings.

Two pictures of world-wide fame illustrate this change, — Raphael's Madonna,

mentioned above, and Perugino's Coronation of the Virgin.   In the first, the entire background is composed of seraphs
and cherubs apparently evolved from thin
blue air, and in constant danger of disap-
pearing in the golden-tinted background.
In the second, the multi-colored wings
of the floating cherubim are beautiful and
the harmony of tones is exquisite, but
they represent an innovation to which one
must become more and more accustomed
as artists are less reverent in their work.

The five angelic choirs which follow the
seraphim and cherubim are not familiar
to us in works of art, although they were
painted with great accuracy in the words
of the mediæval theologians.

When archangels are represented merely
as belonging to their order, and not in their
distinctive offices, they are in complete
armor, and bear swords with the points
upwards, and sometimes a trumpet also.

FRA ANGELICO. — A GLORY OF ANGELS.

Angels are robed, and are represented in accordance with the work in which they are engaged. Strictly speaking, the wand is the angelic symbol, but must be frequently omitted, as when the hands are folded in prayer, or musical instruments are in use, and in a variety of other occupations.

All angels are said to be masculine. They are represented as having human forms and faces, young, beautiful, perfect, with an expression of other-worldliness. They are created beings, therefore not eternal, but they are never old, and should not be infantile. Such representations as can be called infant angels should symbolize the souls of regenerate men, or the spirits of such as die in infancy,— those of whom Jesus said that "in heaven their angels do always behold the face of my Father."

Angels are changeless; for them time

does not exist; they enjoy perpetual youth and uninterrupted bliss. To these qualities should be added an impression of unusual power, wisdom, innocence, and spiritual love.

In the earliest pictures of angels the drapery was ample, and no unusual attitudes, no insufficient robes, nor unsuitable expression was seen in such representations so long as religious art was at its best.

White should be the prevailing color of angelic drapery, but delicate shades of blue, red, and green were frequently employed with wonderful effect. The Venetians used an exquisite pale salmon color in the drapery of their angels; but no dark or heavy colors are seen in the robes of angels in the pictures of the old Italian masters. The early German painters, however, affected angelic draperies of such vast expanse and weighty coloring, embroidery, and jewels, that apparently their angels must perforce descend to earth, and never hope to rise again without a change of toilet.

I shall presently speak of angels in their offices of messengers, guardians, choristers, and comforters. At present I am thinking of the multitudes of angels which were introduced into early religious pictures to indicate a "cloud of witnesses." They lend an element of beauty and of spiritual emotion to the scenes honored with their presence. Their effectiveness has appealed to many Christian architects who have fully profited by the example of Solomon, who "carved all the walls of the house — temple — with carved figures of cherubim," and he made the doors of olive-tree, and he carved on them figures of cherubim.

In the same manner, in many old churches, angels carved in marble, stone or wood, and painted on glass, in frescoes on walls, and in smaller pictures, fill all spaces, and are everywhere beautiful. So long, however, as the stricter theological observances prevailed, angels were not permitted as mere decorations, but were so placed as to illustrate some solemn and significant portion of the belief and teaching of the Church.

Angels were only second to the persons of the Trinity at this period, and preceded the Evangelists. They were represented as surrounding divine beings, and the Virgin Enthroned, or in Glory.

What was known as a Liturgy of Angels was most effective and beautiful. It consisted of a procession of angels on each side of the choir, apparently approaching the altar, all wearing the stole and alba of a deacon, and bearing the implements of the mass. The statues of kneeling angels, not infrequently placed on each side the altar, holding tapers, or the emblems of the Passion of Christ, were not mere decorations, but symbolized the angelic presence wherever Christ is worshipped. In short, either processions or single figures of angels, in any part of a church, and apparently approaching the altar, are symbols of the glorious hosts of heaven who evermore praise God.

During the first three centuries of Christianity the representation of angels was not permissible, and it is interesting to observe the crude and curious manner in which they were pictured in the illuminated manuscripts and the mosaics of the fifth century. Indeed, until the tenth century the angels in Art were curiously formed, and more curiously draped.

Giotto first approached the ideal representation of angels, and, naturally, his pupils excelled him in their conception

of what these celestial beings should be.
It was, however, Angelico who first —
and shall we not say last? — succeeded
in portraying absolutely unearthly angels,
— angels who must have appeared to him
in his holy dreams, and impressed themselves on his pure spirit in such a wise
that with mere paints and brushes he
could picture a superhuman purity.

Not an angel of Angelico's resembles
any man, while in the angels of other
masters, beautiful, seraphic, and charming as they may be, we often fancy that
we see a beautiful boy, or a happy child,
who might have served the artist as an
angel-making model.

Wonderfully celestial as Angelico's angels seem to be, they are feminine, almost
without exception.   In his time this criti-
cism was held to be a serious one; but
since angels are sexless, — according to
the religious teaching on which this

FRA ANGELICO. — AN ANGEL OF THE TABERNACLE.

spiritually-minded monk relied, — I fail to see ground for disapprobation of his work.

The angels of Giotto and Benozzo Gozzoli, with all their beauty, are also feminine, while the great Michael Angelo, whose angels have not yet attained to wings, failed to represent such celestial beings as one would choose as personal attendants.

Leonardo's angels almost grin; Correggio reproduced the lovely children who did duty as his angels; almost the same may be said of Titian; while in the pictures by Francesco Albani, Guido Reni, and the Caracci, the angels are simply attractive and even elegant boys, as may be seen in our illustration of the child Jesus with angels, by Albani. It is so difficult to distinguish the angels of some artists from their cupids, that one can only decide between them by learning the titles of their pictures. These are characteristics of the works of these masters as a whole, with rare exceptions, rather than of single pictures.

To whom, then, may one look for satisfactory angels? For myself, I answer, to Raphael, and especially to his later works. His angels are sexless, spiritual, graceful, and, at the same time, the personification of intelligence and power, as may be seen in our illustration of the Archangel Michael. Witness also the three angels in the Expulsion of Heliodorus from the Temple, in the Stanza della Signatura, in the Vatican. They are without wings, and none are needed to emphasize their godlike wrath against the thief who robbed the widow and orphan in the very temple of the Most High. The celestial warrior on his celestial steed, — believed to be St. Michael, in his office of Protector of the Hebrews, — the deadly mace drawn back ready to strike the fallen robber, and his two rapidly gliding attendants, with streaming hair and swift, spirit-like movement, are such conceptions and personifications of superhuman power as can scarcely be parallelled in any other work of Art.

Rembrandt, too, painted wonderful angels. No adjective ordinarily applied to such pictures is suited to these. They are poetical, unearthly apparitions, and once studied, can no more be forgotten than can some of Dante's and Shakepeare's immortal lines.

Modern artists have, speaking generally, wisely followed the examples of old masters in their treatment of angels. The poet Blake, however, is a notable exception to this rule. He painted angels that surely "sing to heaven," while they float upon the air which their diaphanous drapery scarcely displaces, and seem about to vanish and become a portion of the ether which surrounds them.

I cannot better close this chapter than by quoting what Mr. Ruskin writes of the earlier and later representations of angels.

He says of the earlier pictures that there is "a certain confidence in the way in which angels trust to their wings, very characteristic of a period of bold and simple conception. Modern science has taught us that a wing cannot be anatomically joined to a shoulder; and, in proportion as painters approach more and more to the scientific, as distinguished from the contemplative state of mind, they put the wings of their angels on more timidly, and dwell with greater emphasis on the human form, with less upon the wings, until these last become a species of decorative appendage, — a mere *sign* of an angel.

" But in Giotto's time an angel was a

FRANCESCO ALBANI. — THE CHILD JESUS WITH ANGELS.

complete creature, as much believed in as a bird, and the way in which it would, or might, cast itself into the air, and lean hither and thither on its plumes, was as naturally apprehended as the manner of flight of a chough or a starling.

"Hence, Dante's simple and most exquisite synonym for angel, ' Bird of God; ' and hence, also, a variety and picturesqueness in the expression of the movements of the heavenly hierarchies by the earlier painters, ill-replaced by the powers of foreshortening and throwing naked limbs into fantastic positions, which appear in the cherubic groups of later times."

CHAPTER II.

SAINT MICHAEL.

THE archangels alone have names, and being known to us by them, as well as in connection with certain important events in heaven and on earth, we involuntarily think of them with a more intimate and, at the same time, a more reverent and sympathetic feeling than we can possibly have for the numberless nameless angels of the heavenly choir.

In works of Art, these last are always beautiful, always smiling, and ever ready to appear in greater or lesser numbers whenever any notable religious event is taking place, thus apparently justifying those who believe that we are always surrounded by these celestial beings. They are a most decorative audience of witnesses, and when they are playing upon their musical instruments, or with open lips and upturned, rapturous eyes are singing praises to God, they contribute an enchanting element to the representation.

But the story of the archangels and their wonderful deeds, as told in Scripture and in the sacred legends, impresses us with a vivid sense of their marvellous power and wisdom, as well as of their tender sympathy for the human beings whom they protected and served in their office of guardians and defenders. The official duties that have been assigned them by the theologians have the effect of giving them a place, so to speak, in which we may think of them ; and this

serves to make them more positively exist-
ent to our minds than other angels are.
In comparison with such a personality
as we must involuntarily give to St.
Michael, the hovering, musical angels are
so intangible, such veritable airy visions,
that they elude all practical thought of
them, and appear to be evolved upon
occasion from the air into which they
vanish.

Michael (like unto God) is the cap-
tain-general and leader of the heavenly
host; the protector of the Hebrew nation, and the conqueror of the hosts of
hell; the lord and guardian of souls,
and the patron saint and prince of the
Church militant. His attributes are the
sceptre, the sword, and the scales.

Gabriel (God is my strength) is the
guardian of the celestial treasury; a bearer
of important messages; the angel of the
Annunciation, and the preceptor of the

Patriarch Joseph. His symbol is the lily.

Raphael (the medicine of God) is the chief of guardian angels, and was the conductor of the young Tobias. He bears the staff and gourd of a pilgrim.

Uriel (the light of God) is regent of the sun, and was the teacher of Esdras. His symbols are a roll and book.

Chamuel (one who sees God) is believed by some to be the angel who wrestled with Jacob, and who appeared to Christ during the agony in the garden. Others believe the latter to have been Gabriel. Chamuel bears a cup and staff.

Jophiel (the beauty of God) is the guardian of the Tree of Knowledge, who drove Adam and Eve from the Garden of Eden; the protector of seekers for truth; the preceptor of the sons of Noah; the enemy of those who pursue vain knowledge. His attribute is a flaming sword.

Zadkiel (the righteousness of God) is sometimes said to have stayed the hand of Abraham from the sacrifice of Isaac, while others believe this to have been the work of Michael. The sacrificial knife is the symbol of Zadkiel.

When the archangels are represented merely as such, without reference to their distinctive offices, they are in complete armor, holding swords with the points upwards, and sometimes bearing trumpets also. They are of a twofold nature, since they are powers, as are the princedoms, and fulfil the duties of messengers and ministers, as do the angels.

Although each of the seven archangels has been many times represented in works of Art, I know of no example in which they are seen together, and can be distinguished by name. There are occasional instances of the representation of seven angels, blowing trumpets, which are in-

tended to illustrate the text in Revelation, "And I saw the seven angels which
stand before God, and to them were given
seven trumpets."

In pictures of the crucifixion, and of
the Virgin with the body of her dead son,
— known as the Pietà, — the instruments
of the Passion are frequently borne by
seven angels, and the same number appear in pictures of the last judgment.
But as neither the Eastern or Western
Church acknowledged the seven archangels, it is probable that these pictures
represent the angels of Revelation.

A most interesting example of artistic
symbolism is seen in a picture painted in
1352 by Taddeo Gaddi, and now in the
Church of Santa Maria Novella, in Florence. Here seven angels attend on St.
Thomas Aquinas, and bear the symbols
of the distinguished virtues of this reverend and learned saint. The symbols

are a church — Religion; a crown and
sceptre — Power; a book — Knowledge;
a cross and shield — Faith; an olive
branch — Peace; flames of fire — Piety
and Charity; and a lily — Purity.

The Hebrews believed that Michael,
Gabriel, Raphael, and Uriel sustain the
throne of God. The first three are reverenced as saints in the Catholic Church;
and their divine achievements and celestial beauty have been a fruitful inspiration
to painters and sculptors, resulting in
the creation of many immortal works of
art.

The Archangel Michael is reverenced
as the first and mightiest of all created
beings. He was worshipped by the Chaldeans, and the Gnostics taught that he
was the leader of the seven angels who
created the universe. After the Captivity
the Hebrews regarded him as all that is
implied by the Prophet Daniel when he

RAPHAEL. — THE ARCHANGEL MICHAEL CASTING SATAN
OUT OF HEAVEN.

says, "Michael, the great prince which
standeth for the children of thy people."
It is believed that he will be privileged to
exalt the banner of the Cross on the
Judgment Day, and to command the
trumpet of the archangel to sound; it
is on account of these offices that he is
called the "Bannerer of Heaven."

As captain of the heavenly host, it
devolved on Michael to conquer Lucifer
and his followers, and to expel them from
heaven after their refusal to worship the
Son of Man; and terrible was the punishment he inflicted on them. Chained in
mid-air, where they must remain until
the Judgment Day, they behold all that
happens on earth. Man, whom they dis-
dained, has flourished in their sight, and
wields a power that they may well envy,
while the souls of the redeemed constantly
ascend to the heaven which is closed
to them. Thus are they constantly tor-

mented by hate, and a desire for revenge, of which they must ever despair.

St. Michael is represented in art as young and severely beautiful. In the earliest pictures his drapery is always white and his wings of many colors, while his symbols, indicating that his conquests are made by spiritual force alone, are a lance terminating in a cross, or a sceptre. Later, it became the custom to represent him in a costume and with such emblems as indicated the nature of the work in which he was engaged; and except for the wings, his picture might often be mistaken for that of a celestially radiant knight, since he is clothed in armor, and bears a sword, shield, and lance. But his seraphic wings and his bearing mark him as a mighty spiritual power; and this impression is increased rather than lessened, when in all humility he is in the act of worship before the

Divine Infant, or stands in reverent attitude near the Madonna, as if to guard her and her heaven-sent son.

When conquering Satan the treatment is varied, but the subject is easily recognized. More frequently than otherwise, the archangel stands on the demon, who is half human and half dragon, wearing a suit of mail, and is about to pierce the evil spirit with a lance or bind him in chains.

Such pictures date from the earliest attempts in religious painting, and the same subject was represented in ancient sculpture. Some of these works are so crude as to be absurd, but for their manifest reverence and sincerity. An early sculpture in the porch of the Cathedral of Cortona, probably dating from the seventh century, presents the archangel in long, heavy robes, reaching to his feet; he stands solidly on the back of the dragon, and as if to make the footing more secure, the beast curls his tail in air and lifts his head as high as possible, holding his mouth wide open, into which St. Michael presses his lance without a struggle. The whole effect is that of some calm and commonplace occurrence, and is in striking contrast with the spirit of the conflict which is represented, as well as with the superhuman combat depicted by later artists.

The dragon is personified by a variety of horrible reptilian forms. Some artists even attempted to follow the apocalyptic description. "For their power is in their mouth, and in their tails: for their tails were like unto serpents, and had heads, and with them they do hurt."

Lucifer is not always alone, but is sometimes surrounded by demons, who crouch with him at the feet of St. Michael, before whom a company of angels kneel in adoration.

During the sixteenth century the pictures of this archangel took on the military aspect, to which I have referred, and but for the wings would have represented St. George, or a Crusader of the Cross, as suitably as the great Warrior Angel.

An exquisite small picture of this type, now in the Academy at Florence, was painted by Fra Angelico. The lance and shield and the lambent flame above the brow are the only emblems; the latter symbolizing spiritual fervor. The rainbow-tinted wings are raised and fully spread, meeting above and behind the head; the armor is of a rich dark red and gold. The pose and the expression of the countenance indicate the reserved power and the godlike tranquillity of the celestial warrior, and fitly represent him as the patron of the Church Militant.

The representations of St. Michael conquering Lucifer are so numerous and so interesting technically, that any adequate account of them and of their artistic and theological development would fill a volume, and might be considered rather tiresome. I shall speak especially of two examples which are very generally accepted as the most satisfactory of them all.

The first, painted by Raphael when at his best, is in the Louvre. It was a commission from Lorenzo dei Medici, who presented it to Francis I. The subject was doubtless chosen by Raphael as a compliment to the sovereign, who was the Grand Master of the Order of St. Michael, the military patron saint of France.

It was painted on wood, and sent with three other pictures, packed on mules, to Fontainebleau, where Lorenzo was visiting, in May, 1518. The picture was somewhat injured on the journey. In 1773 it was transferred to canvas, and "restored" three years later, but at the

beginning of this century the restorations
were removed. We must believe that the
picture has suffered from these chances
and changes, but the fact remains that it
is still a glorious work by a great master.

The beautiful young angel does not
stand upon the fiend beneath him, but,
poised in air, he lightly touches with his
foot the shoulder of the demon in vulgar
human form, fiery in color, having horns
and a serpent's tail. The expression of
the angel is serious, calm, majestic, as
he gazes down upon the writhing Satan,
whose face, as he struggles to raise it, is
full of malignant hate. This detail is lost
in the black and white reproductions.

Michael grasps the lance with both
hands, and so natural is the action, so
easy and graceful, that the beholder in-
stinctively waits to see the weapon do
its work, while flames rise from the earth
as if impatient to engulf the disgusting

demon. The head of the angel, with its
light, floating hair is against the background of the brilliant wings, in which
blue, gold, and purple are gloriously min-
gled; his armor is gold and silver; a
sword hangs by his side, and an azure
scarf floats from his shoulders. His legs
are bare, and his feet shod with buskins,
which leave the toes uncovered. The
contrast between the exquisite, angelic
flesh tints, rosy in hue, and the brown
coloring of the demon, effectively empha-
sizes the beauty of purity and the loath-
someness of evil.

The St. Michael of Guido Reni so
closely resembles that of Raphael in gen-
eral treatment, that it is more nearly just
to compare these works than is usually the
case with pictures of the same subject by
different masters. The attitude of Guido's
saint is like that of a dancing-master when
contrasted with the pose of Raphael's,

GUIDO RENI. — THE ARCHANGEL MICHAEL OVERPOW-
ERING SATAN.

and his demon is simply low and base, devoid of malignity or any supreme evil.

But the head and face of Guido's Michael make his picture wonderful; they adequately express divine purity and beauty, while the studied and fictitious qualities of Guido's art — here at their best — serve to enhance the exquisite effect of this angelic warrior, and the picture is justly esteemed as one of the treasures of the Cappucini at Rome.

Outside of Italian art, the St. Michael of Martin Schoen is well worth notice. The figure is fully draped in a long, flowing robe and mantle; the pose is most graceful, and the bearing of the angel dignified and unruffled. The demon is made up of fins, a savage mouth, and numerous claws with which to seize its victims; an entirely emblematic and most repulsive figure.

There are occasional pictures of the

"Fall of the Angels," in which St. Michael contends against the entire company of rebellious spirits. These are illustrative of the text, "When Michael and his angels fought against the dragon, and the dragon fought and his angels, and the great dragon was cast out."

The painting of such a picture at Arezzo, about 1400, caused the death of Spinello d'Arezzo, whose mind so dwelt upon the demons he had painted that he went mad, and fancied that Lucifer appeared to him, and cursed him for having represented the fiend and his angels in so revolting a manner. The horror of the artist induced a fever of which he died.

The smaller of the two pictures of this subject by Rubens, in Munich, is esteemed a miracle of art. It displays the inventive power of the great Flemish master in a wonderful *tour de force*, for the rebel

angels are not fallen, but falling, and
tumbling headlong out of heaven, down,
down, — in such confusion and affright
as only Rubens could portray.

In some cases Raphael and Gabriel are
represented as witnesses of the combat
between Michael and Lucifer. To my
taste, these figures, with their abundant
white draperies, detract from the simplicity and dignity of this impressive
scene. Not only these archangels, but
apostles and saints are sometimes introduced, in spite of the evident anachro-
nism, as observers of this great spiritual
struggle, while hosts of angels are above
and around the picture.

In short, the representations of this
subject, in one form and another, are
almost numberless, and can scarcely be
too many, when they are regarded as
embodying the great truth of the spiritual triumph over evil.

Mrs. Jameson says: " This is the secret of its perpetual repetition, and this the secret of the untired complacency with which we regard it . . . and if to this primal moral significance be added all the charm of poetry, grace, animated movement, which human genius has lavished on this ever-blessed, ever-welcome symbol, then, as we look up at it, we are 'not only touched, but wakened and inspired,' and the whole delighted imagination glows with faith and hope, and grateful triumphant sympathy, — so, at least, I have felt, and I must believe that others have felt it, too."

The representations of St. Michael as the Lord of Souls are less numerous than those of the subjects just mentioned, but are very interesting. In some votive pictures he appears as the protector of those who have struggled with evil, and gained a victory. In such pictures the angel has his foot upon the dragon, or holds a dragon's head in his hand, and bears the banner of victory.

Again, Michael is represented with his scales engaged in weighing the souls of the dead; in such pictures he is unarmed, and bears a sceptre ending in a cross. The souls are typified by little naked human figures; the accepted spirits usually kneel in the scales, with hands clasped as in prayer; the attitude of the rejected souls expresses horror and agony, which is sometimes emphasized by the figure of a demon, impatient for his prey, who reaches out his talons, or his devil's fork, to seize the doomed spirits.

Leonardo da Vinci represented the angel as presenting the balance to the Infant Jesus, who has the air of blessing the pious soul in the upper scale. Signorelli, about 1500, painted a picture of this subject, which is in the church of San

Gregorio at Rome, in which the archangel, in a suit of mail, stands with his
wings spread out, and the balance with
full scales held above a fierce, open-
mouthed dragon. The lance of the
archangel has pierced through the under
jaw of the beast and entered his body,
making an ugly wound, and a hideous
little demon, resting on his tiny black
wings, is clutching the condemned spirits
in the lower scale.

In pictures of the Assumption or Glorification of the Virgin, if St. Michael is
present, it is in his office of Lord of Souls,
as the legends of the Madonna teach that
he received her spirit, and guarded it
until it was again united with her sinless form.

As Lord of Souls it is taught that St.
Michael conducted the spirits of the just
to heaven, and even cared for their bodies
in some instances. The legend of St.

H. MÜCKE. — THE TRANSLATION OF ST. CATHERINE OF ALEXANDRIA.

Catherine of Alexandria teaches that her
body was borne by angels over the desert
and sea to the top of Mount Sinai, where
it was buried; and later a monastery was
built over her sepulchre. In the picture
of the "Translation of St. Catherine,"
which we give, St. Michael is one of
the four celestial bearers of the martyr
saint.

In rare instances St. Michael was represented without wings. Such a figure
standing on a dragon is a St. George,
unless the balance is introduced. When
the archangel stands upon the dragon
with the balance in his hand, he appears
in his double office as Conqueror of
Satan and Lord of Souls. Memorial
chapels and tombs were frequently decorated with this subject, a notable in-
stance being that on the tomb of Henry
VII., in Westminster Abbey.

In pictures of the Last Judgment, St.

Michael is sometimes seen in the very act of weighing souls, and, although I have nowhere found this explanation, it has seemed to me that the souls being thus weighed at the last hour should symbolize those of whom St. Paul said, "We shall not all sleep, but we shall all be changed, in a moment, in the twinkling of an eye, at the last trump: for the trumpet shall sound, and the dead shall be raised incorruptible, and we shall be changed."

Since the Archangel Michael was made the guardian of the Hebrew nation, he was naturally an important actor in many scenes connected with their history. It was he who succored Hagar in the wilderness (Genesis xxi., 17), who appeared to restrain Abraham from the sacrifice of Isaac (Genesis xxii., 11). He brought the plagues on Egypt and led the Israelites on their journey. The Jews and early Christians believed that God spake through the mouth of Michael in the Burning Bush, and by him sent the law to Moses on Mount Sinai. When Satan would have entered the body of Moses, in order to personate the prophet and deceive the Jews, it was Michael who contended with the Evil One, and buried the body in an unknown place, as is distinctly stated by Jude. Signorelli chose this as the subject of one of his frescoes in the Sistine Chapel, and I have seen no other representation of it, although I believe that a few others exist.

It was Michael who put blessings instead of curses into Balaam's mouth (Numbers xxii., 35), who was with Joshua in the plain of Jericho (Joshua v., 13), who appeared to Gideon (Judges vi., 2), and delivered the three faithful Jews from the fiery furnace (Daniel iii., 25). This last subject is one of the earliest in Christian

art, and was a symbol of the redemption
of man by Jesus Christ. There are still
other like offices which St. Michael filled
as the protector of the Jews, while several
important works are attributed to him in
the Apochrypha and in the Legends of
the Church.

For example, in the apochryphal story
of Bel and the Dragon, it is related that
when King Cyrus had thrown the prophet
Daniel into the lions' den, and he had been
six days without food, the angel of the
Lord appeared to the prophet Habakkuk
in Jewry, when he had prepared a mess of
potage for the reapers in his field, and the
angel commanded Habakkuk to carry the
potage to Babylon and give it to Daniel.

"Then Habakkuk said, ' Lord, I never
saw Babylon; neither do I know where
the den is.' Then the angel of the Lord
took Habakkuk by the hair of his head,
and set him in Babylon over the lions'

den; and Habakkuk cried, saying, 'O Daniel, Daniel, take the dinner which God hath sent thee,'—and the angel again set Habakkuk in his own place."

At one period this subject was represented on sarcophagi; but I have only seen it in prints after the Flemish artist, Hemshirk.

In the legends of St. Michael we read that in the sixth century, when the plague was raging in Rome, and processions threaded the streets chanting the service since known as the Great Litanies, the Archangel Michael appeared, hovering over the city. He alighted on the summit of the Mausoleum of Hadrian and sheathed his sword, from which blood was dripping. From that hour the plague was stayed, and from that day the Mausoleum, which is surmounted by a statue of the Archangel, has been called the Castle of Sant' Angelo.

The legends also give an account of two

appearances of St. Michael when he commanded the erection of churches; one at
Monte Galgano, on the east coast of Italy,
and the second at Avranches in Normandy.
The first site was found to cover a wonderful stream of water, which cured many
diseases, and made the church of Monte
Galgano a much frequented place of
pilgrimage.

The church in Normandy is on the
celebrated Mont Saint Michael, and is
famous in all Christian countries. From
the time when the angel appeared to St.
Aubert, the bishop, and commanded him
to build the church, this saint was greatly
venerated in France, and was made patron
of France and of the order which St.
Louis instituted in his honor.

The first church erected here was
small, but Richard of Normandy and
William the Conquerer raised a magnificent abbey, which overlooked the most

Fra Filippo Lippi. — The Annunciation of the Death of the Virgin Mary.

picturesque scenery, and for this reason, if no other, remains a much frequented spot.

The old English coin called an angel was so named from the representation of St. Michael which was stamped upon it.

The pictures of St. Michael announcing to the Virgin Mary the time of her death, bear so strong a resemblance to those of the Annunciation, that it is necessary to remember that these have the symbols of a palm on a lighted taper in the hand of the angel, instead of the lily of the Archangel Gabriel, as is seen in our illustration of a beautiful picture in the Florentine Academy.

The legend relates that on a certain day the heart of Mary was filled with an inexpressible longing to see her Son, and she wept sorely, when lo ! an angel clothed in light appeared before her, saluting her, and saying, " Hail, O Mary ! blessed by

Him who hath given salvation to Israel!
I bring thee here a branch of palm gath-
ered in paradise; command that it be
carried before thy bier in the day of thy
death; for in three days thy soul shall
leave thy body, and thou shalt enter into
paradise where thy Son awaits thy coming." Mary answering, said: "If I have
found grace in thy sight tell me thy name,
and grant that the Apostles may be re-
united to me, that in their presence I may
give up my soul to God. Also, I pray
thee, that after death my soul may not
be affrighted by any spirit of darkness,
nor any evil angel be given power over
me." And the archangel replied: "My
name is the Great and Wonderful. Doubt
not that the Apostles shall be with thee
to-day, for he who transported the prophet
Habakkuk by the hair of his head to the
lions' den, can also bring hither the Apostles. Fear thou not the evil spirit, for

thou hast bruised his head, and destroyed his kingdom." And the angel departed, and the palm branch shed light from every leaf and sparkled as the stars of heaven.

And the duty of the archangel was thus fulfilled until he should again appear as Lord of Souls to receive the spirit of the Virgin, to guard it until it should again inhabit her sinless body.

CHAPTER III.

THE ARCHANGEL GABRIEL.

THE Archangel Gabriel is mentioned by name but twice in the Old Testament. First in Daniel viii., 16, when he explained the vision which the prophet had seen, and again in Daniel ix., 21, when Gabriel appeared to Daniel to give him skill and understanding.

Likewise in the New Testament he is twice mentioned, in Luke i., 19 and 26, when he announced to Zacharias the birth of John the Baptist, and to the Virgin Mary that she was favored of the Lord, and blessed among women. On each of these occasions he filled the office of a

84

messenger or bearer of important tidings.
It is believed to have been Gabriel who
fought with the Angel of the Kingdom
of Persia for twenty-one days, when
Michael came to his relief, and Gabriel
again visited Daniel to strengthen him,
and explain "that which is noted in the
scripture of truth," and to announce that
the king of Græcia should overcome the
king of Persia.   After which Gabriel returned to his battle with the Angel of
Persia.

The contest with the angel of Persia is
a subject which offers unusual opportu-
nities in its artistic representation; it is,
however, much the same in spirit as the
struggle between Michael and Lucifer,
and the preference was given to the latter
by the painters of religious subjects.

St. Gabriel has been many times portrayed as the messenger announcing the
birth of John the Baptist and that of

Jesus Christ. In the apochryphal legends he also foretells the birth of Samson, and that of the Virgin Mary. From these frequently repeated messages which foretold important births, Gabriel naturally came to be regarded as the angel who presides over childbirth.

The great number of representations of the Annunciation to the Virgin Mary make it difficult to select those of which to speak. The earliest pictures of this event portray it with great simplicity, purity, and grace. A spiritual mystery is being depicted, and is handled with sincere reverence and the utmost delicacy.

The scene is usually the portico of an ecclesiastical edifice. When seated, the Virgin is on a species of throne, but she is more frequently represented as standing. The archangel is at some distance from her, not infrequently quite outside the porch. He is majestic and beautiful;

is clothed in white, wearing the tunic and pallium, or archbishop's mantle. His wings are large, and brilliant with many colors, and his abundant hair is bound with a jewelled tiara. He bears either the sceptre of power or a lily in one hand, while the other is extended in benediction. Sometimes he holds a scroll inscribed with the words, " Ave Maria, gratia plena," Hail! Mary, full of grace, which words Dante represents Gabriel as constantly repeating in paradise.

The angel is the chief figure in this scene in the earlier pictures; he is joyfully triumphant, announcing the coming of the Saviour, while the Virgin is all humility and submission; in some cases her head is covered, an extreme expression of lowliness, and she is always self-effacing in attitude and expression.

An early custom in churches was to place the picture of the Virgin on one

side of the altar, and that of the angel
on the other side; or, if both figures
were in the same frame, a division was
made by an architectural pillar, or a con-
ventional ornament between them. In
many cases the Virgin and the Archangel
were placed separately above, or on each
side of some scene from the life of Jesus,
usually an altar piece. The picture by
Fra Filippo Lippi, which we give, is a
very fine example of the so-called "divided Annunciations." It is in the Florentine Academy. This picture is very
beautiful, and fittingly expresses the humility and surprise of the Virgin and the
reverence of the heavenly messenger. It
is also a good example of Fra Filippo's
style; his draperies were graceful, abundant, and usually much ornamented with
designs in gold, of which we have here
enough for elegance, while it is not over-
done as in other works of this artist.

FRA FILIPPO LIPPI. — A DIVIDED ANNUNCIATION.

A very ancient Annunciation, of peculiar and elaborate arrangement, dating from the fifth century, is in mosaic, over the arch in front of the choir in the church of Santa Maria Maggiore, in Rome. The classical treatment of the dresses, and of the entire composition, makes this work so different from the usual conception of the subject as to be worthy of observation. There are two scenes: in the first, the archangel is sent on his mission, and is rapidly flying towards the earth, as if in haste to utter his joyous salutation, "Hail! thou art highly favored! Blessed art thou among women!"

The second scene presents Gabriel standing before the Virgin, who is seated on a throne, behind which are two guardian angels. This representation is so utterly unlike what is known as Christian art as to make a lasting impression, by reason of its classical treatment; all the details have an air of belonging to an earlier period than that known as mediæval, and the figures might be those of ancient Greeks.

It is extremely curious and interesting to observe the various methods of representing the Archangel Gabriel in pictures of the Annunciation. At times he might be mistaken for the ambassador of a proud and powerful earthly potentate. He is clothed in gorgeous raiment, with a rich train, sometimes borne by one, and again by three page-like angels, while he carries himself with majestic haughtiness.

We do not wonder that the difference between the estate of an archangel sent by God, and the humility of the Virgin of Galilee, should have misled some artists; or that with them the angel held the first place, especially as it was only thus that any element of splendor could be intro-

duced into their pictures. Indeed, we
have engravings after a picture by Raphael, in which the Virgin is kneeling
before the angel, who raises the right
hand in benediction.

But the gradual increase in the venera-
tion accorded to the Virgin, and the titles
of Queen of Heaven, and Queen of Angels, which were bestowed on her, soon
changed the spirit of the representations
of the Annunciation; and while the Virgin loses none of her humility and submission, the angel bows, and even kneels
to her, thus emphasizing his acknowl-
edgment of her superior holiness, —
since an archangel could only kneel
before spiritual perfection.

It was well that the patriarchs and
prophets should acknowledge the superiority of the angels sent to them, — but
the glory of the Mother of Christ should
be represented as commanding the rever-

ence of even the highest of created beings
— only thus could the faith of the Church,
for which these religious pictures were
painted, be fittingly illustrated.

Thus it became customary to omit the
sceptre in the hand of the angel, and to
give him the lily alone, or the lily and the
scroll.   Indeed, there are notable pictures
in which Gabriel has no symbol, but with
hands clasped over his breast, and head
inclined, he seems to worship the Virgin
while declaring his mission to her.   There
are, however, few Annunciations in which
the lily does not appear.   It is the special
symbol of the purity of Mary, to whom is
applied the verse from the Song of Solomon : " I am the rose of Sharon, and the
lily of the valleys."   In some pictures the
lily is seen in a vase near the Virgin.

Occasionally the symbol of peace is introduced in pictures of the Annunciation
by placing a crown of olive on the head

ALESSANDRO ALLORI. — THE ANNUNCIATION.

of the archangel, or an olive branch in his hand. Here Gabriel is presented as announcing the " Peace on earth and good will towards men," which Raphael and his attendant angels chanted to the shepherds on the birth of Jesus.

The early German painters were fond of picturing Gabriel in priestly robes, heavily embroidered, and rich in color. This dress supplied the same gorgeous effect as was given by the princely trains of which I have spoken. In these pictures Gabriel usually kneels, — his ample robes falling on the pavement around him, — thus avoiding the proud bearing of the regally vestured messenger.

The simplicity of the scene, when Gabriel is appropriately draped in the filmy white robe, — which is the usual conception of an angel's dress, — is far more satisfactory and harmonious with the spirit of the miraculous Annunciation than any splendid vestments can possibly be.

The earliest pictures of the Annunciation, however, in spite of unsuitable costumes, and of certain technical imperfections, are more acceptable to the reverent mind than are those of a later time, in which the angel is scantily draped and is apparently conscious of his physical beauty, while the Virgin is entirely wanting in grace or dignity. Such a rendering of this scene is most offensive; all the more so that these pictures are frequently well executed, and were they not presented as representations of this sacred subject, but given some appropriate title, they would have claims to a certain artistic approbation.

Other artists, like Allori, in our illustration, represent an all too conscious Virgin, an angel who apparently poses for a picture, and a mass of utterly

inappropriate detail. This Annunciation, which is in the Florentine Academy, affords an excellent example of
this objectionable style, and its faults
are emphasized when it is compared
with the serious dignity of Fra Filippo's
picture and that which follows, by Fra
Angelico. By such comparisons the
great difference between true sentiment
and affectation in Art becomes apparent.

There are some Annunciations in which
the Virgin is represented as starting up
from fear or surprise, quite as one might
fancy that a tragedy queen would do, were
her privacy unceremoniously disturbed.

Again the Virgin Mary is fainting from
emotion, and thus could not have replied
to the angel in the Scriptural words, "Behold the handmaid of the Lord; be it
unto me according to thy word."

Not infrequently, in representations of
this scene, the Holy Spirit, as a dove,

hovers above or near the Virgin, or flies
in through a window; again the Almighty
is seen in the clouds, surrounded by a
celestial light, and sometimes attended by
celestial spirits. In rare instances the Eternal Father sends the Infant Jesus down
from the sky bearing a cross, and preceded
by a dove. These extremely symbolic
Annunciations are usually of an early date.

Fra Angelico painted the Annunciation with intense reverence and simplicity. We have an illustration of his
fresco on the wall of the corridor in
his convent of San Marco, in Florence,
which is, to my mind, one of the most
beautiful and spiritual Annunciations in
existence. It tells the sacred story faithfully; there is nothing introduced that
does not essentially belong here. The
Virgin gives the impression of being
equal to the angel in purity and goodness; he is superior only in knowledge.

FRA ANGELICO.—THE ANNUNCIATION.

Angelico believed that he was divinely directed in his work, which he began with prayer, and for this reason he would never change his original design. His care in the finish of his pictures was phenomenal; his draperies were dignified; his color and composition were harmonious. It has well been said of his works: "Every part contributed to that unity of tenderness, inspiration, and religious feeling which marks his pictures, and which are such as no one man had ever succeeded in accomplishing." Angelico knew nothing of human anxieties and struggles, and could not paint them; he could not depict the hatred of the enemies of Christ; martyrdoms and persecutions were feebly represented by him, but to annunciations, coronations of the Virgin, and kindred subjects he imparted a sweetness and a spiritual fervor that has rarely, if ever, been surpassed. We can imagine him rising from his prayers with his conceptions of the Virgin and the archangel as distinct in his mind's eye as they are to our vision in his pictures, and it is easy to understand that the man who lived in his atmosphere would be void of ambition, and refuse to be made Archbishop of Florence, as he did.

Gabriel is reverenced by the Jews as the chief of the angelic guards, and the keeper of the celestial treasury. The Mohammedans regard him as their patron saint; their prophet believed this archangel to be his inspiring and instructing spirit. Thus he is important in the faith and legends of Christians, Jews, and Mohammedans alike. Milton may have had the Jewish tradition in mind when he represented Gabriel as the guardian of paradise:

" Betwixt these rocky pillars Gabriel sat,
   Chief of the angelic guards, awaiting night."

CHAPTER IV.

THE ARCHANGEL RAPHAEL.

REPRESENTATIONS OF THREE, AND OF FOUR ARCHANGELS.

THE Archangel Raphael is esteemed as the guardian angel of the human race. He especially protects the young and innocent, and guards pilgrims and travellers from harm. It was he who warned Adam of the danger of sin, and declared to him its dread consequences. Milton thus interprets the message:

" Be strong, live happy, and love ! but first of all
Him, whom to love is to obey, and keep
His great command ; take heed lest passion sway
Thy judgment to do aught, which else free-will

Would not admit; thine, and of all thy sons
The weal or woe in thee is placed; beware!"

That Raphael's language was benevolent and sympathetic, as imagined by the poet, appears in Adam's farewell to the angel:

"Since to part
Go, heavenly guest, ethereal messenger,
Sent from whose sovereign goodness I adore!
Gentle to me, and affable hath been
Thy condescension, and shall be honor'd ever
With grateful memory. Thou to mankind
Be good and friendly still, and oft return!"

Representations of St. Raphael are far less numerous than are those of St. Michael and St. Gabriel. They are always pleasing, and present him as a benign, sympathetic, and companionable friend to those whom he serves. His symbol is habitually a pilgrim's staff; as a guardian he wears a sword, and has a small casket or vase, containing the

" fishy charm " against evil spirits. He wears a pilgrim's dress, has sandals on his feet, and a pilgrim bottle or wallet hangs from his belt. His flowing hair is bound by a diadem, and his beautiful face expresses the benevolence of his character and mission.

Many chapels and some churches are dedicated to the Archangel Raphael, as the chief of celestial guardians, and in these are numerous pictures commemorating his benevolent deeds. The greater part of the representations of this archangel are so connected with the history of Tobias, that it is necessary to know his story, in order to enjoy or understand these pictures. I will give this beautiful Hebrew narrative as concisely as possible:

Tobit was a rich man, and just; and he and his wife, Sara, were carried into captivity by the Assyrians. He gave alms to all his people, lived justly, and ate not the bread of the Gentiles. His misfortunes, however, increased; he had but his wife and his son, Tobias, left to him, when he became blind, and prayed for death.

At the same time a man named Raguel, who dwelt in Ecbatane, was afflicted with a daughter who was persecuted by an evil spirit. She had married seven husbands, and each one had been killed by the fiend, as soon as he entered the bridal chamber. The maiden was accused of these murders, and, like Tobit, she prayed for death.

God then sent the Archangel Raphael to cure the blindness of Tobit, and take away the reproach of the unhappy daughter of Raguel of Ecbatane.

At this time Tobit desired his son, Tobias, to go to Gabael in Media to receive ten talents, which Tobit had left in trust with Gabael. Tobias asked,

"How can I receive the money, seeing I know him not?" Tobit gave Tobias the handwriting, and bade him seek a guide for his journey. Raphael then offered to guide the young man, who knew not that he spoke with an arch-angel. Tobias led Raphael to his father, and they agreed upon the wages the guide should receive, and Tobit gave directions concerning the journey, while he and Sara, his wife, were greatly afflicted at parting with Tobias.

At evening the travellers came to the river Tigris, and when Tobias went to bathe, a fish leapt out at him. Raphael told the youth to take out the liver and gall of the fish and preserve it carefully, which being done, they roasted the fish and ate it. When Tobias asked why he should keep the liver and the gall, the angel told him that the heart and liver would cure a person vexed with an evil spirit, if a smoke from them was made before the person; and the gall would cure the blindness of one afflicted with whiteness of the eyes.

In our illustration from the picture by Andrea del Sarto, in the Belvedere, Vienna, Tobias carries the fish, and it appears to represent the moment when Raphael is making his explanation of its purpose.

As they proceeded Raphael said: " Brother, to-day we shall lodge with Raguel, who is thy cousin; he hath but one daughter, named Sara; I will ask her as a wife for thee: she belongs to thee by law, and is fair and wise, and you can marry her when we return." Then Tobias, who knew the fate of the seven husbands, was filled with fear lest he too should die, and thus afflict his parents, who had no other child.

But Raphael assured Tobias that Sara

ANDREA DEL SARTO. — THE ARCHANGEL RAPHAEL
CONDUCTING THE YOUNG TOBIAS.

was the wife that the Lord intended for him, and that when he entered the marriage chamber the evil spirit would flee at the smoke he should make with the liver of the fish, and would never return. When Tobias heard this he loved the maiden, and his heart was effectually joined to her.

When they came near Ecbatane, they met Sara, and she led them to her parents, who rejoiced to see them, and wept when ˙ they heard of the blindness of Tobit. While the servants of Raguel prepared a supper, Tobias said to the angel, "Speak of those things of which thou didst talk, and let this business be despatched." Then Raphael asked Raguel to give Sara to Tobias; but the father was sore distressed, and told of the death of the seven who had already married her; but as Sara belonged to Tobias by the law of Moses, his request could not

be denied, and before they did eat together, Raguel joined their hands, and
blessed them.

Then the marriage chamber was prepared, and the maiden wept; but her
mother comforted her, and when Tobias
entered and made the smoke as the angel
had directed, the evil spirit fled. Tobias
and Sara knelt in thankfulness, and Tobias prayed as Raphael had told him,
and Sara said, " Amen."

In the morning Raguel dug a grave,
for he wished to bury Tobias quickly,
that no one should know what had happened; but when he sent to see if he
were dead, it was found that the young
husband was quietly sleeping. Then
there was great rejoicing, and a wedding
feast was made, which lasted fourteen
days. Meanwhile, Raphael went to Gabael and received from him the ten talents, and when the feast ended, the angel

conducted Tobias and Sara to Tobit, and Raguel bestowed on Sara half his wealth.

As they approached Nineveh, Raphael said to Tobias, "Let us haste before thy wife, to prepare the house: and take thou the gall of the fish." The mother of Tobias was watching for his return, and was greatly alarmed at his long absence. When she saw him with his guide, and the little dog which he had taken away, she ran to Tobit with the news, and they rejoiced greatly. Raphael now said to Tobias, "I know that thy father will open his eyes; therefore anoint them with the gall, and being pricked therewith, he shall rub them, and the whiteness shall fall away, and he shall see thee." And so it was, and Tobit was blind no more, and they all rejoiced and blessed God.

Then Tobias recounted all that had happened, and his parents went out with him to meet his wife, and her servants, and cattle, and all she had brought with her. And the people were filled with wonder to see that Tobit was blind no more, and they rejoiced greatly with him during seven days when he kept a feast.

Tobit bade his son to call his guide and give him more than the wages that had been named. And Tobias wished to give the angel half of all he had brought back with him, and Tobit said, "It is due unto him." But when Raphael knew their intentions he commanded them to glorify God for all his goodness, and told Tobit that his goodness and sorrows and those of the daughter of Raguel had been known in heaven, and God had sent him to heal all these troubles; and added, "I am Raphael, one of the seven holy angels, which present the prayers of the saints, and go in and out before the glory of the Holy One."

Our illustration after the picture of

GIOVANNI BILIVERTI. — THE ARCHANGEL RAPHAEL
REFUSING THE GIFTS OF TOBIAS.

Giovanni Biliverti in the Pitti Gallery, Florence, places before us the scene, when, refusing reward, the Archangel declared himself. The beauty of the angel, the affectionate enthusiasm of Tobias, and the sincere and reverent gratitude of the old Tobit are wonderfully portrayed, while the young wife and the aged mother in the background complete the group of those who have been delivered from their sorrows by the messenger of the Most High.

From the time when the angel left them Tobit and Raguel prospered, and after Tobit and Sara died, Tobias removed to Ecbatane and inherited the wealth of Raguel; he lived with honor to be an hundred and seven and twenty years old, and to hear of the destruction of Nineveh.

Milton thus refers to the story of Tobias:

" The affable archangel
Raphael ; the sociable spirit that design'd
To travel with Tobias, and secured
His marriage with the seven times wedded maid."

Raphael is frequently represented without wings when leading Tobias, who — in order to emphasize the contrast between an angel and a mortal — is made very small, and is thus manifestly out of keeping with the story. When the wings appear there is no reason for dwarfing Tobias, and the picture is far more satisfactory. It is not difficult to discern that if the story of Tobias is considered as an allegory, the young man personates the Christian, guided and guarded through life by God's mercy.

There is, in Verona, in the Church of St. Euphemia, a most impressive chapel which was decorated with pictures illustrating the story of Tobias, by Carotto, a pupil of Mantegna, who seems to have painted more in the manner of Leonardo than in that of his master.

Various incidents of the story are effectively pictured, but the famous altar-piece, the greatest work by Carotto, is the most important of the number. It represents the Archangels Michael, Gabriel, and Raphael, — three exquisite wingless figures, — the latter being in the centre, and the only one having an aureole. He is leading Tobias, and looking down at the youth with an expression of tenderness.

St. Michael is on the right; one hand rests on his great sword, while with the other he lifts his crimson robe. His countenance, serious and indomitable in expression, fitly indicates the characteristics that his titles imply. He is the Lord of Souls and the Angel of Judgment, so far as human imagination can picture so exalted a celestial being.

St. Gabriel, on the left, holding a lily, and gazing heavenward in adoration, is a beautiful, angelic figure, far less powerful than the other archangels, and quite in harmony with his office.

The impression on my mind, made by this picture, is that Gabriel realizes that his blessed office has been fulfilled, his active work is done, and adoration is now his duty and his joy; but Michael and Raphael have still their great missions to perfect; they are still battling against evil, and guiding men in the paths of righteousness.

Carotto was a native of Verona, and his pictures are rarely seen elsewhere. His color is warm and well blended, while his drawing is severe. It is said that he was but twenty-five years old when he decorated the Chapel of St. Raphael, in 1495. He was of a quick wit, and when told that the legs of his angels were

SANDRO BOTTICELLI. — THE ARCHANGEL RAPHAEL.
(FROM A PICTURE OF TOBIAS AND THE THREE ARCHANGELS.)

too slender, he instantly replied, "Then they will fly the easier."

A very famous and wonderful picture of the three archangels with Tobias, by Botticelli, is in the Academy of Florence. The angels of this artist are frequently criticised for a certain stiffness, but their beautiful faces more than redeem any fault in their figures, and have a sweetness and depth of expression that appeals to the heart and makes one forget less important details.

A picture of St. Raphael leading Tobias, in the Church of St. Marziale in Venice, is said to be the earliest remaining work by Titian. For this reason it is most interesting, but it is certainly not so beautiful as that of Carotto, nor as that of Raphael, called the Madonna del Pesce, — the Madonna of the Fish, — in the Madrid Gallery, in which the master pictures the archangel whose name he bore.

Of this last picture Passavant says, "Here Christian poetry has found its highest expression; for it is poetry which touches all nations the most deeply, and beauty alone can give an idea of divinity."

In the famous Madonna del Pesce, the Virgin is seated on a throne with the child; the young Tobias, holding a fish in his hand, and led by the Archangel Raphael, comes to implore Jesus to cure his father's blindness. The Infant Saviour looks at Tobias, while his hand is on an open book which St. Jerome holds before him; the symbolic lion crouches at the feet of the saint. The background of the picture is principally formed by a curtain, but on the right a small opening of sky is seen.

The whole picture is executed in the best style of the artist's mature power, while it is full of the fervent piety of his earlier works. The Virgin is the ideal of purity and loveliness; the child is radiant with divine beauty; the angel is celestial in his bearing and his countenance, while the head of the reverend saint is grand and noble in expression.

Raphael's Madonnas sometimes seem to be but simple domestic women, gifted with beauty; in them no trace of a mystical or spiritual nature appears; but the Madonna del Pesce, like the Madonna di San Sisto, and the Madonna di Fuligno, justifies the eulogy of Vasari, when he says, " Raphael has shown all the beauty which can be imagined in the expression of a Virgin; in the eyes there is modesty, on the brow there shines honor, the nose is of a very graceful character, the mouth betokens sweetness and excellence." The color of the Madonna del Pesce is admirably clear and harmonious, even for this great master.

This Madonna was originally painted for the Church of San Domenico Maggiore, at Naples, in which church a chapel had been erected as an especial place of worship for the numerous Neapolitans who suffer from diseases of the eye; it was not, however, permitted to serve its intended purpose, and has had an interesting history.

It is said that the Duke of Medina, when Viceroy of Naples, took the picture from the Dominicans without the consent of the government, and when the prior complained to the Pope, Medina had him escorted to the frontier by fifty horsemen, and expelled from the kingdom. In 1644 the Duke took the Virgin with the Fish to Spain, and Philip IV. placed it in the Escurial. In 1813, when the French were compelled to leave Spain, they took this picture, with many others, to Paris.

It was painted on a panel and was in bad condition, and Bonnemaison was commissioned to transfer it to canvas. This work was not completed in 1815, when other pictures which had been taken from Spain were returned, and this Madonna remained in France until 1822. Naturally, it must have lost something of its original excellence, but it still holds a place of honor in the wonderful Italian Gallery of the Madrid Museum; it is a rival of the famous Dresden Madonna — di San Sisto — in the regard of many connoisseurs in art.

The various scenes from the story of Raphael and Tobias have been represented in the works of artists of all nations. Rembrandt four times painted the parting of Tobias from his father and mother, and several other incidents in the story. His picture in the Louvre, of the departure of the Archangel, is

remarkable for its spirited action. As
the angel ascends, flying through the
air, he seems to part the clouds as a
strong swimmer passes through the
breakers of the sea.

There have been many curious conceits introduced into some of the early
religious pictures, and I have seen two
instances in which little seraphim and
angels are perched on trees, near the
Virgin and Holy Child. The idea seems
to be that these " Birds of God " — as
Dante calls the angels — are making
music and singing for the Divine Infant, some of them also praying for his
solace.

Occasionally a series of pictures called
the Acts of the Holy Angels has been
painted. It consists of eleven strictly
Scriptural subjects, usually as follows,
but varied in some instances by the introduction of other motives of the same

character, as, for example, the angel appearing to Hagar and to Elijah :

   I. The Fall of Lucifer.
  II. The Expulsion of Adam and Eve from the Garden of Eden.
 III. The Visit of Three Angels to Abraham.
 IV. The Angel Preventing the Sacrifice of Isaac.
  V. The Angel Wrestling with Jacob.
 VI. Jacob's Dream.
VII. The Deliverance of the Three Children from the Fiery Furnace.
VIII. The Angel Slays the Host of Sennacherib.
 IX. The Angel Protects Tobias.
  X. The Punishment of Heliodorus.
 XI. The Annunciation to the Virgin.

I have already said that of the seven archangels to whom Milton refers, when he says :

            " The Seven
Who in God's presence, nearest to his throne,
Stand ready at command,"

but three are recognized by the Christian Church ; and when three archangels are

seen together, they are Michael, Gabriel,
and Raphael.   In the Greek Church this
representation is regarded as typical of
the military, civil, and religious power,
and, accordingly, the costumes indicate
a soldier, a prince, and a priest.

But Uriel has not been entirely ignored,
even by the Christian Church, and an
early tradition teaches that this archangel,
and not Christ, accompanied the two disciples on their way to Emmaus.   In the
book of Esdras we read, " The angel that
was sent unto me, whose name was
Uriel."   His office was that of interpreter
of judgments and prophecies, which Milton recognizes thus:

"Uriel, for thou of those Seven Spirits that stand
In sight of God's high throne, gloriously bright,
The first art wont his great authentic will
Interpreter through highest heaven to bring."

In several ancient churches four archangels are represented in the architectural

decoration. An example in which they are very splendid is that in the mosaics above the choir arch in the Cathedral of Monreale, Palermo. These colossal, armed figures are impressive, not only from their size, but also because of their apparent realization of their illustrious rank in the order of created beings.

More frequently the four archangels are so represented as to appear to sustain the roof, or vault, in churches where the figure of Christ, or his symbol, the Lamb, is pictured as the central decoration. These are clearly intended to personate the four "who sustain the throne of God." Their symbols are sceptres or lances; at times they stand erect, like faithful, watchful guardians; again with arms outstretched they seem to uphold the vault on which Christ is portrayed.

The representations of three archangels are more numerous than the above, and

are variously treated. In some ancient
pictures they have no wings, and appear
like men of princely rank and noble character. I have seen the visitors of Abraham
thus represented, which accords with the
Hebrew idea of angels at the period when
Abraham was thus honored; for, as I have
mentioned, it was not until after the captivity, when the Egyptian custom of giving
wings to their representations of messengers had been observed, that the cherubim
and seraphim covered the mercy-seat with
their wings.

One of the best known and most beautiful pictures of these angelic visitors is that
by Raphael in the fourth arcade of the
Loggie of the Vatican.

CHAPTER V.

GUARDIAN ANGELS, ANGEL CHORISTERS, AND ADORING ANGELS — DEMONS AND EVIL SPIRITS.

FROM the classification of the angelic hosts by the early theologians, and the special duties assigned to each class, we learn that the word angels, as ordinarily used, refers to archangels and angels only; these two classes are associated with human life in all its phases, while princedoms protect monarchies, thrones sustain the throne of God, cherubs continually worship, and seraphs adore the Most High.

A belief in guardian angels — those especially devoted to the care of indi-

viduals — is far more widespread than
the realism of the present day is inclined
to admit. The godly man has a sure
warrant for this trust in the ninety-first
psalm :

" Because thou hast made the Lord, which is my
refuge, even the Most High, thy habitation; there
shall no evil befall thee, neither shall any plague
come nigh thy dwelling. For he shall give his
angels charge over thee, to keep thee in all thy
ways."

We cannot think of angels as a reality
in the winged, human forms that have
been given them in Art, any more than
we can look for mermaids to rise from
the waters mentioned in the charming
legends in which these maidens acted
their parts. These imaginary and apparently palpable angels are but allego-
ries, which long have been and continue
to be the angels of Art, and we could not
willingly give them up. We know that

FRA ANGELICO. — ANGEL CHORISTERS.

they are impossible, even fantastic, if we permit ourselves to be matter-of-fact; but as emblems of spiritual guardians, sent to mortals by an ever-watchful Father, we love them; and we wish to believe in guardian angels for those who are dear to us, even if we cannot realize them for ourselves.

In one of the early councils of the Church the form of angels was considered, and it was maintained by John of Thessalonica that they were in shape like men, and should be thus represented. This decision is supported by the supposition that God spoke to the angels when he said, "Let us make man after *our* image;" and again by Daniel, when he describes his heavenly visitors as "like unto the similitude of the sons of men."

A guardian angel must be ever beside his charge from the beginning to the end of life, not only to guard from evil, but also to incite to good. In sorrow he is a comforter; in weakness, strength; even in death he is faithful, and contends against the evil spirits who fight for the possession of every soul; and after death he bears the spirit to St. Michael, the Lord of Souls. Thus is the guardian angel represented in Art, as is seen in our illustration called the Angel of Peace.

When we observe a beautiful, unselfish life that rises far above its surroundings, we recall the belief in angelic guardians, and the description which Milton gave of a chaste, saintly soul:

> " A thousand liveried angels lackey her,
>   Driving far off each thing of sin and guilt;
>   And in clear dream and solemn vision
>   Tell her of things that no gross ear can hear,
>   Till oft converse with heav'nly habitants
>   Begin to cast a beam on th' outward shape."

The impersonality of angels is one of their most precious qualities. An angel

KAULBACH. — THE ANGEL OF PEACE.

is never active except as the agent of the Almighty, deputed to manifest his mercy and love to the pious, or to inflict his punishments on the wicked. Thus angels must be perfect beings; and while they love to serve, their service is void of the personality which is inherent in all human service. When they sing together it is because some good has come to men, and when they mourn it is for human affliction.

According to the teaching of the Fathers of the Church to which we have referred, the combat between good and evil angels is unceasing, and they also warrant Christians in invoking the aid of angels, and believing them to be ever near to prevent evil and encourage good. From the views of the early theologians the artists evolved their manner of representing the hosts of heaven, and while for a time angels were represented as colossal, gradually they became more graceful and lovely, as well as more human.

An ideal, a thought, must be personified to be represented to the eye, and I doubt if any new personification of angels could satisfactorily replace that which has been developed in Art during sixteen centuries, and to which we are accustomed from our earliest childhood. The angels that are known in pictures, watching over children, preventing harm to individuals, as in the sacrifice of Isaac, encouraging or even compelling worthy action, as in the case of Balaam, are dear to the heart of the world.

The representations of guardian angels in the more homely relations, watching sleeping infants, guiding their feeble steps, — as is seen in our frontispiece, — and shielding them from accidents, are modern.   To the end of the sixteenth century guardian angels, while engaged in all these minor duties, according to the teaching of the Church, were only represented in Art as performing solemn and superhuman deeds.

This may have resulted from the fixed belief of the old artists in these angelic beings, and their deep reverence for them, while modern artists are simply seeking a graceful and poetic subject. But, be this as it may, the angels who perform miracles to prevent the torture of Christian martyrs and other superhuman acts, are as essentially guardian angels as are those bending over cradles and gathering blossoms for children in the fields.

After the guardians, the choristers, or musical angels, most appeal to us. They are beautiful in their representations, and fulfil an ideal mission. Their hymns of praise are not all devoted to the pure worship of the Almighty, — except as he is all and in all, — since they rejoice and sing when blessings are conferred upon mankind.

How exquisite is the story in the second chapter of St. Luke's Gospel, when the single angel announces the birth of Jesus to the shepherds, "and suddenly there was with the angel a multitude of the heavenly host praising God, and saying, 'Glory to God in the highest, and on earth peace, good will toward men.'" In the final sentences of this heavenly chant we have the assurance that angels delight to sing of happiness to mankind.

There is much that appeals to our imagination in the thought of these heavenly musicians. We fancy their perfect instruments attuned to perfect voices, creating such harmonies as no earthly orchestra can reproduce.

> "The harp, the solemn pipe
> And dulcimer, all organs of sweet stop."

PERUGINO. — MUSICAL ANGELS.

In the early days of Christian Art,
painters and sculptors alike delighted in
the representation of musical angels, and
it is surprising to find in how many
scenes they are not only appropriate but
indispensable. Our illustration, after
Perugino, is from his picture of the
Assumption of the Virgin in the Florentine Academy.

They are most fittingly present at the
coronations of Jesus and the Virgin; they
gladly welcomed the just to heaven; they
join in the hymn of St. Cecilia, which
they must have inspired; they are always
in harmony with pictures of the Madonna
and child, and, in short, numerous as
are the representations of them, they are
never too many.

It would seem that certain sculptors
and painters must have seen these blessed
beings in visions, and listened to their
music, so wonderfully did they embody

them in statues and on canvas. Della Robbia, Ghiberti, Fra Angelico, Ghirlandajo, Melozzo da Forli, Vivarini, Gian Bellini, Raphael, Palma, must all have seen, at least with the eyes of the spirit, the angelic choirs which make so precious a part of their legacy to us.

The difference in the sentiments with which these angelic choristers seem to be inspired lends them a peculiar charm. Now they are alone intent on solemnly praising God; again they seem full of such overflowing joy as can only be expressed in vocal harmonies, in symphonies with viol, pipe, harp, and lute. Nowhere are these angels more lovely than when, with their sweet faces turned to the Infant Jesus, they chant their love for him.

Cherubim and seraphim are technically the adoring angels, as they are represented in pictures of God, the Father. But adoring angels are frequently seen in

pictures of the Madonna and Child, as
well as in scenes from the lives of Jesus
and the Virgin. Sometimes they appear
in great numbers, as in Angelico's picture
of the Last Judgment; or in smaller
groups, as the three adoring angels by
Francesco Granacci; or singly, as in the
case of the angel with bowed head,
who stands behind the Virgin in the
Madonna and Angels, by Boticelli; the
last three pictures being among our
illustrations.

Mourning angels appear more frequently in sculpture than in painting, and
are much used as monuments to the dead;
but there are pictures in which angels
show their sympathy with sorrow and
suffering. While from their nature they
cannot be unhappy, they are not represented as joyful in pictures of the Crucifixion and other sorrowful scenes in the
lives of Jesus, the Virgin, or saintly

martyrs. They hide their faces, wring their hands, and manifest their sympathetic grief in various ways. I recall a picture of a mourning angel kneeling before a crown of thorns with tears upon his face.

There are occasional pictures of kneeling angels, who have the appearance of praying. Artists have naturally manifested their individuality in their works, but I do not recall any Scripture warrant for representing angels as themselves praying, although they are present with mortals who pray. It is, however, not inconsistent with their mission to bear the prayers of mortals to the throne of God and to return with a blessing.

In the early centuries of the Church there was a well-established belief that wicked spirits had power over men and tempted them to all manner of sins; they especially desired, it was taught, to lead

Francesco Granacci. — Angels in Adoration.

the pious to revolt against the true religion, and to become idolaters, as they had
themselves revolted against the Almighty.
It was also believed that good and evil
spirits constantly contended over every
human being, the struggle between angels
and demons being unending.

Devils are introduced in many pictures,
and are easily recognized by their demo-
niacal appearance. Frequently they are
very small and numerous. They are
represented as hovering above death-beds,
they rejoice in the persecution of the
martyrs, and wherever seen, are the very
personification of all that is repulsive and
loathsome.

The most important pictures in which
the devil is represented as a human being
are scenes in the temptation of Jesus,
when he was led into the wilderness to be
tempted forty days. Shakespeare says
that " the devil hath power to assume a

pleasing shape," but apparently artists have not recognized this. In their pictures of him there is always some characteristic which at once discloses his personality. His skin is an ugly brown, or the hoofs which he endeavors to hide are disclosed, or the repulsive expression of his face warns one of his dangerous character.

Happily such pictures are not numerous, but an ideal of the repulsiveness of the Father of Lies has been conceived by many from the famous representations of him by Raphael and Guido, in their pictures of his conquest by St. Michael. In numerous cases, however, the presence of Satan is indicated by symbols. The dragon and the serpent are the usually accepted emblems of the Evil Spirit, but there are many variations of this symbolism. A horrid dragon head with open mouth typifies hell. Frequently the serpent has an apple in his mouth and thus personates the wily tempter of Mother Eve; but in many cases the serpent has no relation to the fall of man, and is personified evil.

CHAPTER VI.

PICTURES OF ANGELS AS AUTHORIZED
BY THE SCRIPTURES.

ESIDES the representations of angels in art in accordance with the imagination of individual artists, there are two important classes of angelic subjects, one of which rests upon the authority of the Scriptures, and the other upon that of the sacred legends. A comprehensive treatment of these works would require several volumes of the size of this book; but I will here give a suggestive outline of them.

The first mention of angels in the Old Testament occurs in the third chapter of Genesis, when it is related that cherubims

were placed at the east of the Garden of
Eden, to keep the way to the Tree of Life.
Good pictures of this subject are as rare
as they are beautiful. In them the exquisite garden, the radiant cherubim, and
the dazzling light from the flaming sword,
combine in producing a glorious effect.

In connection with the story of Abraham, angels frequently appear. The sacrifice of Isaac is always an interesting
subject, symbolizing, as it does, in the
submission of Isaac, that of Jesus, and
in the willingness of Abraham to give
his son in sacrifice, that of the Divine
Father to give his well-beloved Son for
the salvation of men. The appearance
of the angel to prevent the consumma-
tion of the sacrifice has been painted
many times, notably by Andrea del Sarto,
whose poetical pictures of this scene are
in the Dresden and Madrid galleries.

The picture by Rembrandt is powerful,

and painfully realistic. It is in the Hermitage at St. Petersburg. The same scene in the Church of Santa Maria della Salute, Venice, is by Titian, and is among the famous works of this great master.

Our illustration after a picture by Il Sodoma, in the Cathedral of Pisa, is in the best style of that master, who has been called the pride of the Sienese school. His acknowledged power to render intense feeling is seen in the face of Abraham, while the angel is an example of his conception of beauty; the submissive Isaac, missing the pressure of his father's hand from his shoulder, without changing his position, turns his eyes to discover the reason for the delay of the expected blow.

In the story of Hagar an angel twice appears, and one is surprised that these charming subjects have so rarely been

IL SODOMA. — THE SACRIFICE OF ABRAHAM.

painted, while the more disagreeable expulsion of Hagar from the home of her youth has been frequently represented; the picture of this scene by Guercino, in the Brera at Milan, is famous, and certainly tells the story of " Cast out the bondwoman and her son " with directness; but there is an element of vulgarity in it that so detracts from its good qualities as to make one wonder that it could have been so much admired.

A far more tender subject is that which pictures Hagar in the wilderness alone, and repentant of her fault, for which Sarah had chastened her; it is at this moment that the angel appears and commands her return to Abraham. A fine example of this rare subject by Pietro da Cortona is in the Belvedere, at Vienna. Rubens also painted this scene.

A picture that is even more pathetic

represents Hagar and Ishmael in the wilderness of Beersheba. Ishmael is fainting from thirst, and Hagar flings herself to the ground with the prayer, " Let me not see the death of the child," when an angel appears to comfort her, and guide her to a hidden spring. The pathos of this scene must appeal to every mother, and a picture of it by Rembrandt is so fine that one can but regret that it is not in a public collection.

The visit of the three angels to Abraham is also a rare subject in Art. I have already referred to that painted by Raphael, in the Vatican. Murillo also represented it in a picture now in a private gallery in England. In neither of these pictures have the angels wings.

The three beautiful figures by Raphael, however, are not like any men whom we have seen; they impress one as beings of another and a far higher sphere than

ours.   Murillo, on the contrary, shows
us three ordinary travellers, and but for
the title of the picture, we should not
suspect that these men were celestial
visitors.   A large picture of this subject by Rembrandt is one of the treasures
of the Hermitage.

Jacob's dream, with the ascending and
descending angels, is an exquisite motive
for illustration, and has been variously
pictured.   A single angel sometimes
watches the sleeper, as if to inspire his
dream and bring him a blessing; again,
there are many angels, and again, but a
small number, who move here and there,
up and down, imparting a remarkable
effect of airy, graceful motion.   The
ladder, too, is widely varied, being represented by one or several flights of steps,
ascending to the clouds.

In the sixth arcade of the Vatican loggie is Raphael's third and best representa-

tion of this dream. Here Jacob's face is turned towards the ladder, on which are six angels; Jehovah appears above with outstretched arms, and surrounded by a glory. It is not one of the best of Raphael's works, and, indeed, all representations of Jacob's dream that I have seen, are, to my mind, insufficient when compared with that of Rembrandt, in the Dulwich gallery. This is a poem as essentially as it is a picture. A stream of dazzling light forms the ladder, up and down which float mystic, radiant angels. The whole impression is so like a dream, so intangible, and yet so apparent, that one wonders how Rembrandt, who so often dwelt upon the all too solid elements of his motives, here caught the innermost spirit of this most spiritual subject.

" The Comforting of Elijah " is a subject with rare possibilities, but has been seldom represented.

Rubens painted a picture of this scene as symbolical of the Lord's Supper, the angel presenting to Elijah the bread and a chalice. Following a custom of some landscape painters who introduced a subject — mythological, historical, or Scriptural — into their pictures, Paul Potter represented the "Comforting of Elijah" in the foreground of one of his pictures. It also occurs in some ancient illuminated Bibles.

William Blake's illustration of the text in Job, "When the morning stars sang together, and all the sons of God shouted for joy," is famous for the unusual character of the angels. Like many pictures by this poet, who was esteemed as half mad, it has an element of other worldliness which is rarely seen in works of his era. Of this especial picture Mrs. Jameson wrote: "His adoring angels float rather than fly, and, with their half liquid draperies, seem about to dissolve into light and love; and his rejoicing angels — behold them — sending up their voices with the morning stars, that, singing, in their glory, move."

The Vision of Ezekiel, in the Pitti Gallery, in Florence, is, so far as I know, a unique representation of this subject. Raphael painted it for Count Ercolani in Bologna. It is mentioned as early as ' 1589, in the Inventory of the Tribune, and has been engraved and copied many times.

Jehovah is represented seated in a glory of cherubim's heads, which are almost unnoticeable by reason of the exceeding brightness illustrative of the text, " And I saw as the color of amber, as the appearance of fire round about within it, from the appearance of his loins even upward, and from the appearance of his loins even downward. I saw as it were the appearance of fire, and it had brightness round about." In accordance with this text also, Jehovah is nude in the upper portion of the figure, the lower portion being draped in purple. Near the Jehovah are the four animals symbolic of the evangelists, the cherub, the lion, the ox, and the eagle, not earthly creations, but mysterious and spiritual as they float along bearing the Messiah, while two small angels are near with outstretched arms.

The sky effects of this wonderful picture are fine; the gray clouds are rolling away, as if for the purpose of disclosing the vision. This picture has been criticised on account of the nude figure of Jehovah; it has been said to be a more proper representation of Jupiter than of the Almighty, but Raphael is justified by the text itself.

Perhaps no representation exists which

more acceptably renders the symbolic nature of the Four Beasts than does this. The exact imitation of nature, which appeared later in works of Art, is entirely opposed to the true meaning of these emblems, which was sacred and mystical. The cherub typifies St. Matthew, because his Gospel sets forth the human nature of Christ more forcibly than the divine. The lion was appropriate to St. Mark, because he first speaks of " the voice of one crying in the wilderness," typical of the lion. The ox belongs to St. Luke, since he dwells on the priesthood of Christ, the ox symbolizing sacrifice; the eagle to St. John, as the emblem of his inspiration, by which he wrote so sublimely of the divinity of Jesus.

There are several other explanations of these symbols which are so often seen in works of Art. But in this especial picture of the " Vision of Ezekiel," it would seem

as if the throne of the Son of Man is composed of these mystic beasts, while the
angels are attending him, and gaze into
his face, as if watching for some service
to be rendered.

When the Four Beasts are so pictured
as to recall those who were full of eyes
within, and rest not day and night, saying, "Holy, holy, holy, Lord God Almighty" (Revelation iv., 7), they fulfil
the intention of the symbol of the early
Church, as it was understood by those to
whom it was sacred. But when, in the
hands of an irreligious and realistic artist,
they become "as the beasts of the field,"
his work is but a travesty upon the mysterious religious symbols, which he thus
debases.

The New Testament gives us a clearer
idea of the nature and offices of angels
than we obtain from the Hebrew Scriptures. We learn of their great numbers

from the words of Jesus, " Thinkest thou
that I cannot now pray to my Father,
and he shall presently give me more than
twelve legions of angels ? " (Matthew xxvi.,
53), and from Paul, when he speaks of the
"innumerable company of angels." In
the Gospels of St. Matthew and St. Luke
we learn that they are superior to human
affections, and not subject to change.
"For in the resurrection they neither
marry, nor are given in marriage, but
are as the angels of God " (Matthew
xxii., 30). " Neither can they die any
more; for they are equal unto the angels " (Luke xx., 36). By the words of
Jesus, however, we are assured of the
sympathy of angels in all that concerns
our spiritual good. In Luke xv., 10,
Jesus says, " Likewise I say unto you,
there is joy in the presence of the angels
of God over one sinner that repenteth."

The belief that angels bear the souls of

MELOZZO DA FORLI. — AN ANGEL.

the redeemed to heaven, rests largely on
the declaration by St. Luke that " the
beggar died, and was carried by the angels
into Abraham's bosom ; " and in Hebrews
i., 14, St. Paul teaches that they are "sent
forth to minister for them who shall be
heirs of salvation."

In the annunciations of the birth of
John the Baptist and of Jesus, the angels
were the messengers of God, as they so
frequently were when they appeared in
the Old Testament.

That angels are attendant on Christ is
taught in the declaration of St. Matthew
that " the Son of man shall come in the
glory of his Father with his angels."
And again, " When the Son of man
shall come in his glory, and all the holy
angels with him."

That angels are deputed to perform
such acts as make for the accomplish-
ment of Christ's mission is shown in

Acts v., 19, when an angel liberated the
Apostles from prison, and commanded
them to "speak in the temple to the
people all the words of life."

When writing to the Romans, St. Paul
speaks of angels, principalities, and powers, thus enumerating the different orders
of angels, and declares their inability to
separate us from the love of God, thus
implying that they can do nothing that
does not accord with the will of the
Almighty, — that they have no power in
themselves. Again, in writing to the
Colossians, St. Paul speaks of things
"visible and invisible," and enumerates
thrones, dominions, principalities, and
powers, while to the Ephesians he declares that God has placed Christ above
all these orders of celestial beings.

After the annunciations to Zacharias
and the Virgin Mary, an angel next appears, in the New Testament story, to

instruct Joseph concerning the miraculous conception of Jesus. The appearance to the shepherds follows, of which I have spoken in connection with the subject of angelic choirs.

Again, Joseph was warned by an angel to flee into Egypt with Mary and the young Child, to escape the anger of Herod. In ancient series of pictures illustrating the life of St. Joseph, this scene was curiously portrayed, and but one modern painter, so far as I know, has been moved to represent it. In the Belvedere, in Vienna, there is an admirable Dream of Joseph, by Anton Raphael Mengs.

Pictures of St. John the Baptist in the wilderness are variously treated, and when he is represented as very young, he is attended by ministering angels. This treatment is warranted by the legend which teaches that he was a mere child of seven or eight years, and is supported by the word of St. Luke in the last verse of the first chapter of his Gospel, " And the child grew, and waxed strong in spirit, and was in the deserts till the day of his shewing unto Israel."

The pictures of the Baptism of Christ are numerous, and the number of attendant angels is varied from two to four, as a rule, although there are examples with even a larger number. Raphael, Verrocchio, Paul Veronese, Francesco Albani, Perugino, Tintoretto, and many others painted fine pictures of this subject, which, besides its great interest from its importance in the life of the Saviour, affords an opportunity for the representation of a beautiful landscape. The picture by Rubens excels in this regard; and in his magnificent setting he has a group of about thirty figures, producing the gorgeous effect which characterizes his work, but failing to suggest the divinity of Christ, or the devotional feeling of the works of Raphael or Verrocchio, and entirely lacking the tenderness of Lorenzo di Credi.

The Bible also contains various texts which authorize a belief in the existence of Satan and his demons. Isaiah exclaims, "How art thou fallen from heaven, O Lucifer, Son of the Morning." St. Matthew speaks of the devil and all his angels, and many other Biblical expressions warrant us in believing that the Spirit of Evil with his attendants is ever tempting men to sin, thus plainly warranting the Fathers in their teaching, to which we have referred.

It is not possible to picture the Temptation of Christ in an attractive manner. Satan has been represented in various monstrous and repulsive forms by some artists, while others have given him such disguises as might well deceive an ordinary mortal. He has thus been presented in the garb and with the bearing of a venerable peasant, and again as a monk with robe and cowl, but his especial symbols usually manifest themselves, in spite of all disguises.

The picture by Ary Scheffer, in the Louvre, which our illustration reproduces, tells the story of the temptation very simply and directly. The style of this painter, sad and almost hopeless, is well suited to subjects of this nature. The contrast between the perfect serenity of the Saviour, and the hideous anxiety and determination of Satan, renders this representation as acceptable as so unlovely a subject can be made.

In Perugino's famous picture in the Sala del Incendio, in the Vatican, Jesus and Satan are seen in mid-air, like a vision, while in the background, sur-

Ary Scheffer. — The Temptation of Christ.

rounded by a dazzling light, another
figure of Jesus is seen between two
ministering angels, while the whole scene
is encircled by a multitude of cherubim
and angels.

In some pictures of this subject angels
are represented as if waiting to support
the Master when he shall turn from the
demon, but far more attractive than these
are the representations in which Satan
does not appear, and angels minister to
Christ in the wilderness, as if illustrating
these beautiful lines :

" They in a flowery valley set him down
    On a green bank, and straight before him spread
    A table of celestial food — divine
    Ambrosial fruits, fetched from the Tree of Life —
    And from the fount of life celestial drink.
        And as he fed, angelic quires
    Sang heavenly anthems." '

One of Murillo's splendid works was
founded on the account of the pool at

Bethesda, as given in John v., 2–8. This was a favorite subject for hospitals, and Murillo painted it for a hospital in Seville, from which it was stolen by Marshal Soult.

In the foreground are Christ, the lame man, and three Apostles; in the background is the pool with its fine porches, above which, in a glorious, dazzling light, the angel hovers, as if about to descend to stir the waters.

It is a magnificent example of the wonderful power of Murillo. The beauty and tenderness of the head of Christ, and the graciousness of his whole bearing, affect the beholder as do few representations of our Lord. The atmosphere is soft and translucent, the angel gently floats rather than flies, and the porches, while not too ornate, impart a dignified balance to the scene. The coloring is such as is peculiar to Spanish art, rich and subdued in contrast with that of the Italians. For example, the red robe and blue mantle, so familiar in pictures of Christ, are here replaced by a rich violet color, most harmonious with the sentiment of the scene.

There is an ancient picture of this subject in a church near Bologna, supposed to be the work of two artists, Jacopo Avanzi, and Lippo d'Almasio. In the same city, in the Church of San Giorgio, is the picture by Ludovico Caracci, which is, to say the least, very decorative, and has been generously praised by some writers on Art. Many representations of the pool of Bethesda are in hospitals, — as, for example, that by Sebastian Conca at Siena, — rather than in galleries; for this reason it is less familiar than are many other scenes in which angels are represented.

There are some subjects too sacred in

their character and too spiritually subtle
in their significance to be adequately pictured to the eye. One of these, to my
mind, is the Agony in the Garden of
Gethsemane. It has, however, appealed
to many artists, and one must admit
that the night scene, the sleeping disciples, the suffering Christ, the consoling
angel, the approaching traitor, and the
dimly discerned city of Jerusalem afford
unusually picturesque elements for an
effective picture. All these have been
artistically treated, but The Divine, the
central thought in the scene, can scarcely
be satisfactorily expressed.

A most surprising error that has frequently been made in pictures of this
subject, is that of giving undue prominence to the sleeping disciples. Their
figures are often placed in the very foreground, as if the spectator should chiefly
consider the unfortunate somnolence of

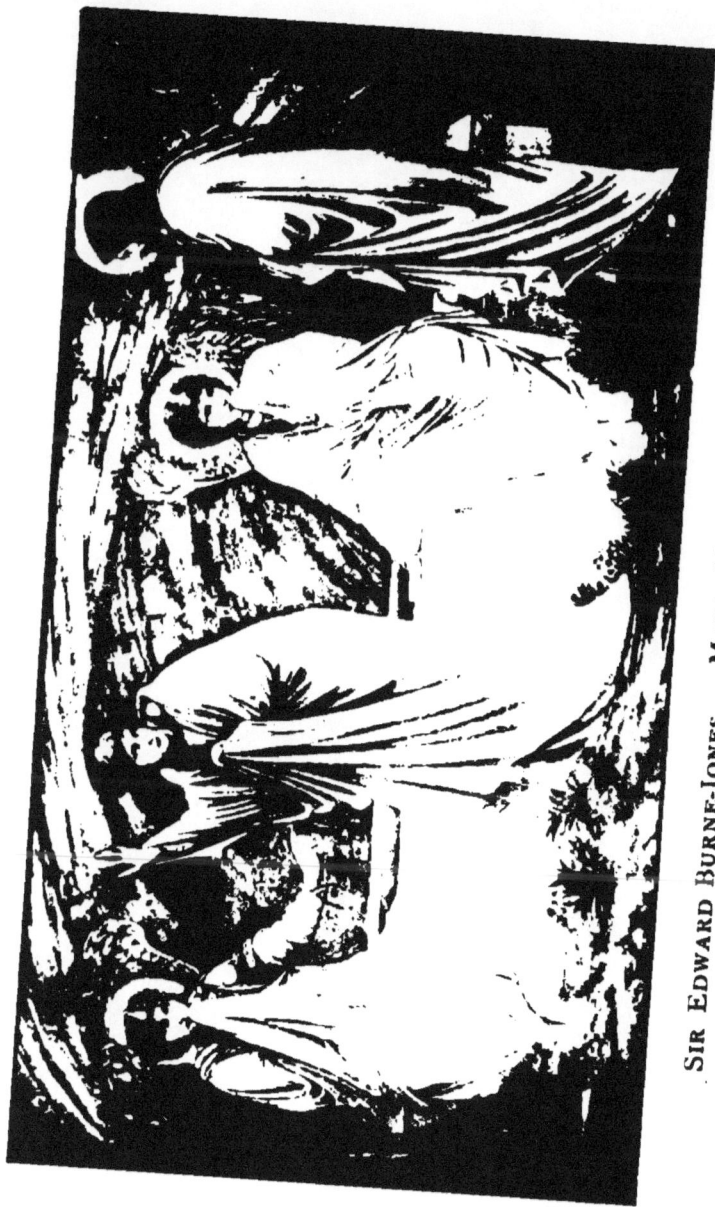

SIR EDWARD BURNE-JONES. — MARY MAGDALENE AT THE SEPULCHRE.

these men; by which means the figures of Jesus and the angel are made to appear as secondary. I have seen no picture in which the sleeping disciples are satisfactorily introduced, and I greatly prefer certain curious ancient representations of the Agony, in which Christ and the angel only are present.

Many famous artists, from the time of Mantegna, have painted their conceptions of the wonderful scene in the Garden. Correggio has at least made Jesus the chief person, and his angel is apparently suited to his office of a comforter. Paul Veronese, Albert Dürer, and Rembrandt have all painted powerful pictures of this subject, and Ary Scheffer has depicted the Agony of Christ with living vividness; but one and all of these works fall so far short of one's highest conception of this wonderful event, that, except as examples of the design, coloring, and

manner of these masters, they appear to
me of little value.

The visit of the women to the sepulchre of Christ is variously represented,
as would naturally result from the different accounts given by the Evangelists.
Some pictures represent Mary Magdalene
alone, when she saw two angels sitting
where the body of Christ had lain, and
almost immediately beheld the risen Lord
near by, as in our illustration after
Burne-Jones. Again, the other women
are pictured who saw two men in shining
garments, and were told, " He is not here,
but is risen;" more frequently the three
Maries are represented coming to the
sepulchre, bearing spices, and finding the
guards paralyzed with terror, and an
angel who tells them that the Lord is
risen.

These scenes have been represented
in Art from its earliest and rudest be-

ginning, and were rendered with perfect simplicity, strictly following the clear scriptural account. Later, the guards were omitted, and the whole scene took on a more dramatic air, until, in the sixteenth century, this subject was rarely painted, and has not again resumed its earlier importance. It makes one in a series of subjects illustrating the life of Christ, but is rarely seen as a separate work. Annibale Caracci painted a picture of the Women at the Sepulchre, which is now in the Hermitage at St. Petersburg; and in Siena there still exists an example of the same subject by Duccio, who lived in the thirteenth century.

Pictures of the Last Judgment, as usually painted, are illustrative of a combination of scriptural teaching with the imaginative suggestions of preachers, writers on religious subjects, poets, and artists,

and elements from the sacred legends.
There is no scriptural warrant for the
presence of Satan and his demons in
this scene, horribly effective and impressive as they are; but I have reason
to think that this element is thought-
lessly accepted as authoritative by many
who interest themselves in religious art.

This subject was not represented in
sculpture or painting before the eleventh
century, and but rarely after that until
three centuries later, when it was wonderfully portrayed, notably by Orcagna,
in the Campo Santo at Pisa.

The portions of these pictures for
which there is scriptural authority are
important. Christ is the Judge in accordance with his own words, Matthew
xvi., 27: "For the Son of man shall
come in the glory of his Father with
his angels; and then he shall reward
every man according to his works." And

still more emphatically in Matthew xxv., 31–46, where the word-picture of the Judgment is a vividly realistic description of some artistic representations of this scene.

The Apostles seated on each side of Christ are also warranted by his words in Luke xxii., 30: " That ye may . . . sit on thrones judging the twelve tribes of Israel." The Virgin, St. John the Baptist, patriarchs, prophets, and saints are all admissible on the authority of St. Paul, who says, I. Corinthians vi., 2: " Do ye not know that the saints shall judge the world ? " And in the following sentence: " Know ye not that we shall judge angels ? "

The angels are deputed to "gather together his elect from the four winds," Mark xiii., 27, and those who fill this office are the trumpet angels in all these representations.

The division of those to be judged rests
on Daniel xii., 2: "And many of them
that sleep in the dust of the earth shall
awake, some to everlasting life, and some
to shame and everlasting contempt;" and
even more positively on Christ's words in
Matthew xxv., already referred to.

In the utter absence of scriptural warrant for the picturing of the devil 'and
his satellites, who seize, torture, and hurl
into hell those doomed to shame and
endless contempt, what defence of it can
be made? Certainly none from an artistic standpoint; and this consideration
should have prevented such representations. Artists should be commiserated
who could not sufficiently express the
woe of the condemned by the wretched-
ness of their faces and manner, as, hearing
the fatal " Depart from me, ye cursed, into
everlasting fire, prepared for the devil and
his angels," they go to the left, not dar-

Fra Angelico. — An Angel conducting a Soul to Heaven.

ing to raise their eyes to Christ, nor even to look at the blessed of his kingdom.

It would be a pleasure to consider separately the different methods of representing the Judge of all the world and those surrounding him, as seen in the works of the masters, but we are here concerned with the angels alone, of which, in nearly all these pictures, there are three classes.

The angels who hold the cross, scourge, nails, crown of thorns, and other symbols of the Passion of Christ, emphasize the theological teaching that men are judged according to their acceptance or rejection of the Atonement by Christ for the sins of the world. In early pictures of the Judgment these angels stand on clouds, below the Judge, but later they were depicted as hovering above the Judgment Seat. In whatever position they are placed, they appear to attribute a

vast importance to the prominence of
the symbols of the Passion. Fra Angelico happily places a single angel at the
feet of Christ with the cross alone, as a
complete symbol of the suffering and
death of Jesus.

The trumpet angels vary in number
from two to many, and are differently
placed according to the varying designs
of the artists. Orcagna and Fra Angelico
placed them below the Judge, thus indicating that their sound could be heard in
all the earth. In other pictures, they sound
the trumpets directly above the graves,
which open, displaying the rising dead,
startled from their long sleep and strug-
gling to gain a foothold on the earth above.

The third class of angels are those who
announce their fate to all who are to be
judged. They sometimes hold the balance in which souls are weighed; again,
they direct those who come to judgment

to the right or left, as in our picture from
the Last Judgment by Fra Angelico, in
the Florentine Academy; and, again, as
in Orcagna's great picture in the Campo
Santo at Pisa, a grand warrior angel, with
splendid wings, — a true St. Michael, —
clad in full armor, with his sword by his
side, a glorious halo about his head, and
the angelic flame above his brow, holds
out two scrolls, — one of joy and one of
woe, — on which are written the names
of the entire human race.

The pictures of the Last Judgment
by Orcagna, Angelico, and Signorelli, in
the Cathedral of Orvieto, and Michael
Angelo, in the Sistine Chapel, are among
the famous pictures of the world.

The Scriptures mention still other appearances of angels, as that to Cornelius,
when he was directed to send to Joppa
for Peter; and, again, when Peter was
in prison and the Church prayed for him,

an angel led him forth and the Apostle departed to Cesarea for safety.

Philip was sent by an angel to meet the Ethiopian eunuch, and teach him the truth, after which he baptized the eunuch, and was then caught away by the Spirit, or angel of the Lord.

At times the angels were sent on missions of punishment, as when Herod, in the midst of his blasphemy, was smitten by God's messenger, and gave up the ghost.

These subjects are rich in artistic suggestion, and nearly all have been represented in painting or sculpture. The book of the Revelation, too, abounds in visions of angels, from the beginning, when an angel from heaven "signified it" to John the Divine, to the end, when the angel refused to be worshipped, and declared himself the fellow servant of John, and of the prophets, and of all that keep the sayings of the book.

FRA BARTOLOMMEO. — AN ANGEL PLAYING THE VIOLIN.

CHAPTER VII.

PICTURES WHICH ILLUSTRATE BOTH SCRIPTURE AND LEGEND.

IN whatever light one may regard the sacred legends of the early Church, it is not possible to understand the representations of angels in Art without some knowledge of these ancient traditions. One who knows nothing of them, finds himself strangely puzzled and disconcerted, before the almost numberless legendary subjects which he sees in churches and galleries.

For example, if one knows nothing of the legend of St. Catherine of Alexandria, how can he explain the picture of her mystic marriage to the Infant Jesus, which

typifies her renunciation of all earthly
things, and her complete dedication of
herself to the service of Christ and his
Church ?

St. Catherine is habitually represented
with a wheel beside her.   When the
wheel is whole, it is a symbol of the
torture with which she was threatened
by the Emperor Maximin; when broken,
it is a token of the miracle by which she
was saved from a horrible death.

During the many years that have passed
since my first visit to the gallery of the
Louvre, I have retained a vivid remem-
brance of my discontent before the beautiful picture of St. Margaret.   The pleasure
that I should have taken in the lovely
face and exquisite figure of the saint, in
the graceful drapery, and other details of
this celebrated picture, was utterly lost
through my ignorance.   I did not know
why she was standing on the frightful

LORENZO DI CREDI. — AN ANGEL IN ADORATION.

dragon, with his horrible mouth wide open, and his terrible claw raised as if to clutch the beautiful maiden.

As a consequence of this experience, I resolved to study the religious symbolism of the early Christian Church, as I had already studied that of the religion of the classic ages. How frequently now, as then, I meet those who perfectly understand the significance of the head of Medusa, or the lyre of Orpheus, who have no conception of the reason for the representation of a church in the hand of St. Jerome, or of the serpent in the chalice of St. John the Evangelist.

There are numerous pictures, in which angels are introduced, that are founded on the Scripture story, but do not follow it strictly. Many subjects are so suggestive of the presence of angels, that there is a legitimate artistic license for introducing them into these scenes.

For example, the Scripture account of
the ministration of angels to Jesus, after
the Temptation and after the Agony in the
Garden, naturally suggests their presence
on other occasions of his suffering, and renders their introduction quite permissible.

Thus, in the picture of Christ after the
Flagellation, in the Monasterio Maggiore
in Milan, by Luini, which is full of the
wonderful tenderness of that master, there
is no angel; while Velasquez, in his picture of the same subject, which is in a
private collection in England, introduces
such a presence.

So in the story of the Ecce Homo no
angel is mentioned, and the usual devotional picture represents the half figure of
Christ, or the head alone, wearing the
crown of thorns. The historical picture
portrays the scene before Pilate, with a
number of figures. Some artists, however, have presented this subject differ-

ently, as in the picture by Moretto, in the Museo Tosi in Brescia.

This shows the Saviour seated upon the steps of a building, probably that in which was the "common hall," in which the soldiers crowned him. He still holds the reed sceptre, though his hands are bound; the cross is on the ground before him, and his head is bowed upon his breast. On the steps behind him, and a little above, stands a weeping angel, holding the garment of Christ as if about to wrap it around him. The expression in the convulsed face of the angel is remarkable. It is as if he endeavored to restrain his tears, but could not. A much later picture by Landelle, called the Angel of Tears, is similar to that of Moretto in sentiment; in it a weeping angel kneels before a crown of thorns, his tears falling over his cheeks.

Angels are also represented in pictures

of the Crucifixion; in fact, they were never absent in the earliest pictures of this subject, although they were but few in number, and were extremely realistic in their treatment, being precisely like ordinary men with wings added to their shoulders. Later their number was largely increased, and they became less human and extremely passionate in the expression of their sorrow in beholding the agony of Jesus. Giotto and Cavallini introduce an element of absurdity into this momentous scene, by representing extremely human little angels as tearing open their plump little breasts in their despair.

This extreme realism was sometimes carried to the extent of picturing angels with chalices, catching the blood which flowed from the hands and side of Jesus. In accordance with true symbolism, a female figure, impersonating the Church, should hold the chalice to the side alone.

From a Copley Print, copyright, 1897, by Curtis and Cameron.

FRENCH. — DEATH STAYING THE HAND OF THE SCULPTOR.

Duccio da Siena, a generation earlier than Giotto, displayed a more subtle perception, and grouped a numerous company of angels in a half circle above the cross, in his famous picture of the Crucifixion, which is one of the treasures of his native city. Two of them kiss the dead hands; others cover their faces; some have thrown themselves down prone upon the clouds; while still others, as if mindful of their duties as messengers, are flying upwards to bear the news to the courts above.

In a few Crucifixions, in which the three crosses appear, angels are receiving the soul of the penitent thief, while demons quarrel over that of the unrepentant criminal. Unpleasant as this treatment is, it is the logical result of the belief that a good or bad angel attended every death, and bore the soul to St. Michael for judgment, as is depicted in many ancient

works of art.   The spirits of the blessed
are tenderly carried skyward, but the
translation of lost souls is attended with
some revolting details.

Gradually fewer angels were represented
at the Crucifixion, and an apparently un-
written law limited them to two or three
with chalices; indeed, for a time this scene
was far less frequently pictured.

Luini and Gaudenzio Ferrari, Lombard
painters of the fifteenth century, again
portrayed so many angels, and such numberless little winged heads, that the upper
portions of their Crucifixions were alive
with them.   These artists, with their re-
fined tenderness of manner, created angels
that have rarely, if ever, been excelled in
what may be termed a genuine angelic
quality.   Especially is this true of Gaudenzio; the lamenting angels above his Crucifixion, in the church at Varallo, are among
the most satisfactory representations of

angels that occur in any picture of this scene.

If the Resurrection of Christ is to be represented, the angel is appropriately present; but as no account of the scene is given in the Bible, and no one witnessed it, each artist who portrayed it was at liberty to give his imagination full play in his work. For a long time there were no pictures of this subject, its treatment being confined to carvings in ivory, on shrines and other small objects. The greater number of artists apparently esteemed it as too sacred, as well as too tremendous, a subject to be adequately conceived and satisfactorily presented.

So far as I can learn, the Resurrection was first painted by Giotto, as one of a series of small pictures upon a press for the sacred vessels in the Church of Santa Croce in Florence; it is now in the Academy of that city. In this picture there is no angel. Fra Angelico represents the Maries talking with the angel, while Christ is suspended in air above them. By degrees the designs for this subject were modified, until, in the picture in the Vatican which has been attributed to Perugino, the rising Christ, bearing the banner of victory, is worshipped by two angels. This work is now believed to be by Raphael, as his authenticated studies for it are in the Oxford Collection.

Perhaps it is to be regretted that the illustration of this supremely mystical subject was ever attempted in Art. I cannot imagine that any existing picture of it should be seriously approved as a whole, although certain figures or details may be sincerely admired.

The Ascension of Christ is another mystical subject, which was long unattempted in a realistic portrayal of the

scene as described in the New Testament. Ancient ivories show Jesus as
grasping the hand of God extended to
him through the clouds, and being thus
drawn up from earth. In the twelfth and
thirteenth centuries the Scripture expression, "he was taken up," was given a
literal meaning, and the figure of Jesus
was represented in the mandorla, — the
oblong glory in which Christ, the Virgin,
or saints are represented when ascending
to heaven, — which was borne by angels
to a certain height, when a cloud received
him out of sight.

As with the Resurrection so with the
Ascension, Giotto was bold enough to
attempt representing the scene in accordance with the scriptural description, and
painted his idea of it on the walls of the
Arena Chapel, in Padua. In the centre
of the lower part of the picture are two
angels, who, with raised hands, direct the

attention of the kneeling Virgin, and groups of Apostles, also kneeling, to Christ, already soaring far above them, accompanied by numerous worshipping angels, who are on both sides, at some distance apart from him.

This fresco is much injured, but is highly valued for the sublimity of its composition. No angel aids Christ to rise. He is apparently able to fulfil his own words, " And I, if I be lifted up from the earth, will draw all men unto me."

Many pictures of the Ascension are seen in galleries, and it became a favorite subject for the decoration of church vaults and cupolas, especially in Greek churches. Correggio's Ascension, in the Church of San Giovanni, in Parma, is famous wherever Christian art is studied. This master depicted numberless little angels flying here and there, riding on clouds or mischievously peeping from behind them, chasing each other as in some boisterous game, and by their levity and frolicsomeness destroying all seriousness of effect, in spite of the solemnity of the Evangelists and Reverend Fathers in the angles of the vault below.

This picture must not, however, be taken as irreverent. Evidently Correggio wished to convey the idea that the Ascension of Christ was an occasion of joy to the angels, to whom his earthly pilgrimage and sufferings had given a certain seriousness, — not sorrow, because angels are happy, and not subject to human wants and weakness.

Now the great work was accomplished, and even the angels were rejoicing that the Son should again resume his place at the right hand of the Father, until the time when he should come again with glorious majesty to judge both the quick and the dead.

One readily perceives how rich a field for the artistic imagination these mystical subjects presented. But in a comprehensive study of them, it is curious to note the effect upon works of Art of the dogmas of the theologians, as they were promulgated from time to time. In some cases, especially in Spain, rules were prescribed for the manner in which religious subjects should be represented, and no artist dared depart from them.

In the representations of angels, however, there was a larger liberty than in the doctrinal subjects of religious art, and to this we owe the possession of many precious works of sculptors and painters, which are never outgrown, and of which we never weary.

ROSSETTI. — THE ANNUNCIATION.

CHAPTER VIII.

ANGELS IN PICTURES OF THE VIRGIN MARY.

THE pictures of the Madonna, or Virgin Mary, may be divided into two classes; the devotional, which illustrate the doctrines or teaching of the early Church, and the historical, or the representation of the actual scenes in the life of the Mother of Christ.

When the Virgin is represented wearing a crown or bearing a sceptre, and attended by worshipping angels, she is in the character of the Queen of Angels. The earlier examples of these pictures, as seen in the Florentine Academy, and in the Churches of Santa Maria Novella and Santa Croce in Florence, are charming in their simplicity, and represent a majestic and mystical womanhood, which entitles them to consideration as works of Art. But later, especially in the seventeenth century, these pictures degenerated into portraits of the self-conscious, unintelligent prettiness of the models from whom they were painted. This subject was a favorite one with certain decadent artists, and the contrast between the most ancient and the later pictures of it, gives one a strong impression of the lack of reverence or ideality in men who could thus represent that holy woman, whose heart found expression in her beautiful hymn, beginning, " My soul doth magnify the Lord," St. Luke i., 46. These pictures have neither the humility, the intellectual power, nor the sublime faith which the face of the Virgin Mary should express.

A favorite devotional picture was the

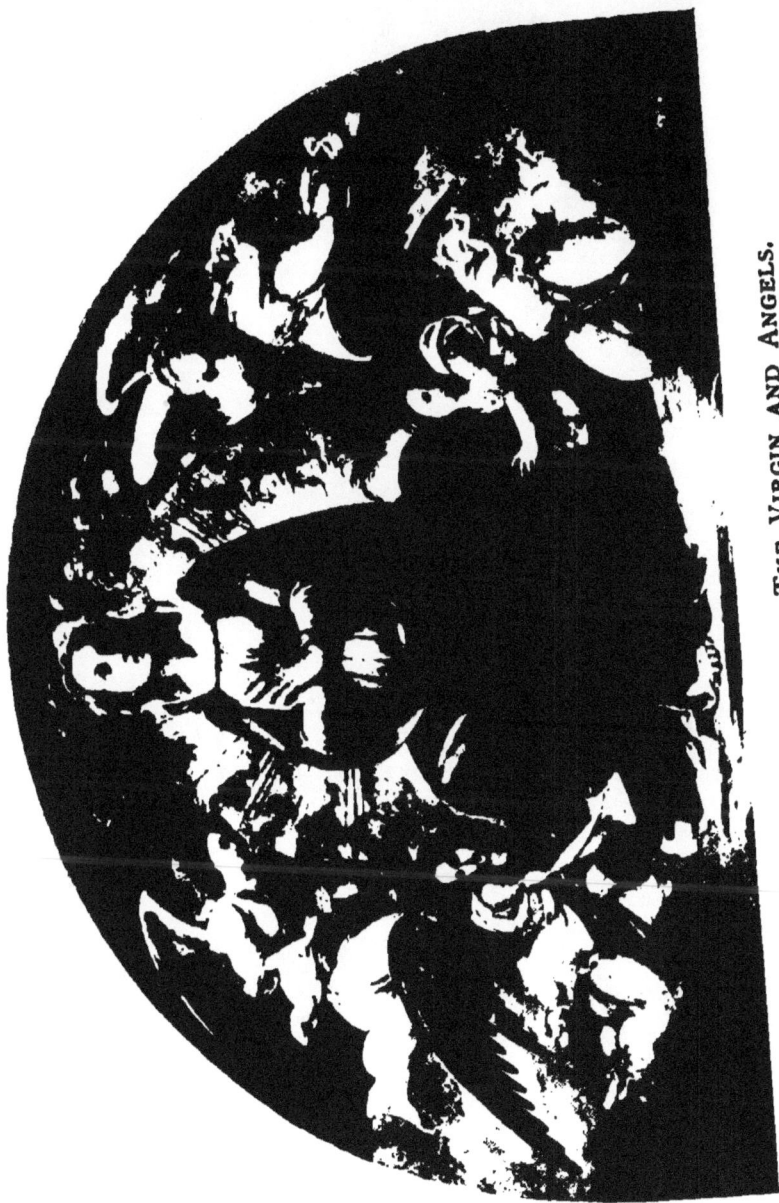

FRANCESCO GRANACCI.—THE VIRGIN AND ANGELS.

Coronation of the Virgin. This representation is an emblem of the Church Triumphant, and is one of the most beautiful, as it was one of the most approved, of the Middle Ages. It appeals to all hearts, since it pictures the reunion of the Mother and Son in heaven, after their separation by his death, and shows him no longer despised and rejected, but reigning in the fullness of power, and exalting his mother above men and angels, welcoming her to his throne, and placing a glorious crown upon her head.

In the most ancient Coronations, which are very interesting, no angels appear. From the time of Giotto, — the beginning of the fourteenth century, — however, angels were witnesses of this scene. Fra Angelico's Coronation, in the Louvre, in which the Virgin kneels to be crowned, has a group of musical angels on each

side. One of the most interesting pictures of this subject that I have seen is
in the Academy of Venice, by Vivarini,
an artist of the island of Murano, who
lived in the fifteenth century.

It is a very large picture, having a
throne in the centre, magnificently ornamented and upheld by six pillars on a
splendid pedestal. Christ and the Virgin
are seated on the throne, he already
crowned, and engaged in placing the
crown on the head of Mary. The celestial dove hovers between them, and the
Heavenly Father appears above, and rests
a hand on the shoulder of each. Above
are nine choirs of angels; nearest are the
glowing seraphim and cherubim having
wings but otherwise so indistinct as to
be formless; above these are thrones,
holding the globe of sovereignty; to the
right are dominations, virtues, powers,
and to the left princedoms, archangels,

and angels. In the lower portion of the same picture are prophets and Patriarchs with the Hebrew Scriptures, the Apostles with the Gospel, saints and martyrs, virgins and holy women, lovely children bearing the cross, nails, spear, and crown of thorns, and the Evangelists and Fathers of the Church. There are at least seventy heads in this picture without the angels; the children are beautiful, and all are finished with great delicacy and care. It is an invaluable example of symbolic art, as well as an exponent of an entire system of theology.

The Coronation was often a most splendid picture, as it warranted the use of magnificent draperies and other accessories. It was also a joyous picture. Every figure introduced had an air of happiness, and the angels were especially glad.

In the picture known as the Mother of Mercy, the Virgin is often attended by

angels.   In ancient pictures and bas-
reliefs of this subject, she was frequently
standing and wearing a long, full cloak,
like that of St. Ursula, which was held
aside by two angels, thus disclosing groups
of kneeling suppliants, praying to her for
mercy.

Very often in this picture the Virgin
holds the Infant Jesus in her arms.   In
other fine examples, — notably in the mas-
terpiece of Fra Bartolommeo, in the Church
of St. Romano, in Lucca, — the figure of
Christ surrounded by angels is seen in
the clouds, as if he aided in these works
of compassion.   Such pictures are numerous in hospitals and charitable institu-
tions, especially in those that are in the
care of the Order of Mercy, where they
are singularly appropriate.   A bas-relief
above the entrance to the Scuola della
Caritas, in Venice, is a fine example of
this subject.

Pictures of the so-called Pietà, represent the Virgin holding the body of the dead Christ on her knees. The greatest artists whose works are known to us have represented this subject in sculpture and painting. When it is a strictly devotional work, the Virgin, the Christ, and mourning angels are the only figures admissible. There are many examples in which there are no angels, the Mother being alone with the dead Christ.

The Pietà by Francia, in the National Gallery, is very beautiful in sentiment, and in execution is full of the tenderness of this master. The Christ is supported by two angels, and the Virgin, with an expression of anguish, seems to look at the beholder as if beseeching sympathy.

In the sublimely pathetic marble group, by Michael Angelo, in a chapel of the Vatican, there are no angels, but we have engravings of another Pietà by this master, in which the Virgin sits at the foot of the cross, her eyes raised and her arms extended towards heaven, while two angels support the Christ, seated lower down, and leaning against the knees of the Virgin. According to the custom of Michael Angelo, these angels have no wings, but their expression is such as would make it impossible to mistake them for earthly children.

There were no pictures of the Immaculate Conception of the Virgin Mary until the seventeenth century, when Spanish and Italian artists vied with each other in representing this subject, and these works may be said to abound in angels.

When the Virgin stands on the moon with full sunlight surrounding her, and wearing the crown of twelve stars, she is the personification of the woman described in the twelfth chapter of the Book of Revelation.

FRANCESCO FRANCIA. — A PIETÀ.

The dogma of the Immaculate Conception of the Virgin was much in favor with the Spanish Church before its confirmation by the bull of Pope Paul V. in 1617, which was welcomed in Seville, not only by the most solemn religious services, but also by the booming of cannon, and the celebration of bull-fights, tournaments, and banquets. Spain and all its colonies were placed under the protection of the Immaculate Conception. Even now, almost three centuries after this event, it is not unusual for Spaniards to use the salute, "Ave Maria purissima!" the response being, "Sin peccado concepida!"

Not long after the publication of the bull, Pacheco laid down rules for the repsentation of this subject in Art, which have been conscientiously followed. The Virgin is very young, her hair golden, her robe white, and her mantle blue. The angels near her bear roses, lilies, and palms. She stands on the moon, wears the starry crown, and the vanquished dragon is beneath her. As the Franciscans were always enthusiastically devoted to this dogma, it was usual to represent the girdle of the Virgin by the cord of the Franciscans.

Murillo, the painter of this subject *par excellence*, was not strictly bound by Pacheco's rules. He adhered to the colors prescribed for the drapery; he varied the tint of the hair, and often was not careful to represent the cord of St. Francis. He never omitted the moon, but it was sometimes full rather than in the crescent, and he pointed the horns upward, while Pacheco directed them to point downward; and he usually omitted the starry crown. But so satisfactory were Murillo's Immaculate Conceptions that he was never accused of being unorthodox.

MURILLO. — THE IMMACULATE CONCEPTION.

Other pictures of the Madonna, by this great Spanish master, are wanting in the characteristics which he invariably gives the Virgin in this subject. Others are commonplace, and might be duplicated among Spanish peasant women; but the Virgin of his Conceptions are ideal. Spotlessly pure, full of grace and repose, exquisite in refinement and delicacy, her hands folded on her breast, and her sweetly serious eyes raised as in prayer, she seems a fitting companion to the angels about her, but all unsuited to the sufferings of the life before her.

Murillo painted this picture twenty-five times, and no two of these works are exactly the same, although the differences are sometimes slight. The angels are so numerous that they seem to fill all space, and to be coming forward in still greater numbers out of the depths of the sky. If the dragon is there, he is concealed by these lovely, spiritual attendants on the queen of their order.

Guido Reni painted several pictures of this subject which was well suited to the master of the Aurora, and afforded full play to his ideal of beauty, and his delicacy of execution.

But it was in the Spanish school that these pictures were multiplied, and this is not strange when we remember that every candidate admitted to the academy of painting in Seville was required to declare his full belief in " the most pure conception of Our Lady."

Mr. Stirling, in his handbook of Spain, speaks of a Conception by Roelas, painted before the time of Murillo, which he calls " equal to Guido." Velasquez also painted a fine Conception, probably before the rules of Pacheco were known, as the Virgin's robe is violet, and she has no unusual beauty. It is, however, a solemn and remarkable work in the bold, early style of this great artist.

In the ancient pictures of the Enthroned Madonna there are always attendant angels; in some later works they are omitted. In this subject the Madonna holds the Infant Jesus on her lap, and is surrounded by angels. The earliest Enthroned Madonnas represent the Virgin seated between the Archangels St. Michael and St. Gabriel, as symbolic of life and death. This representation dates from the eighth century in the carved ivories of the Greek Church, and was repeated in sculpture and glass painting during six or seven hundred years.

Later St. Gabriel appears in the Annunciation only, but as St. Michael was the guardian of Jesus and his mother in their earthly life, he is often beside them, as well as St. Raphael, the guardian spirit of all human beings. Perugino presents both these guardian archangels in his lovely picture in the National Gallery.

This is one of the rare examples in which the three archangels are seen together, each with his appropriate symbol.

In the usual picture of this subject the Madonna is literally enthroned, her throne being rich and decorative. Raphael, however, placed her on the clouds, the child standing beside her, and the angels below, rather than above them. This might be called the Madonna in Glory, although she is seated on the clouds as on a throne.

Angels were represented as attendant upon the Virgin very early in the history of Art. Even the ancient mosaics of Ravenna show them about her throne, and as her office of Queen of Angels

SANDRO BOTTICELLI. — MADONNA AND ANGELS.

came to be more and more considered, angels were represented as adoring her, sustaining her throne, and performing a variety of services, the most charming being that of the musical angels.

When Art reached the height of the fifteenth century, the angelic choristers were exquisite in beauty and in sentiment, as they knelt or stood near the Virgin, or sat upon the steps of her throne, playing upon lute and pipe, or singing as only angels can.

There are so-called half-length En-throned Madonnas, in which the Virgin and Child and angels alone appear. Occasionally the Infant St. John the Baptist is introduced in these pictures, as in the illustration here given, after Botticelli.

The picture known as the Mater Ama-bilis, in which the Madonna caresses the Child, or tenderly gazes at him, rarely has the angelic attendants, but Gian Bellini filled the background of such a picture with winged cherub heads.

There are two classes of pictures of the Madonna and Child, in which the little St. John Baptist is present. When St. John adores Jesus, kisses his feet, or in any way seems to recognize his superiority, it is a purely devotional picture, while a great number of others are simply domestic, friendly scenes. In all of these angels appear in varying numbers.

An exquisite picture, by Filippino Lippi, shows the kneeling Virgin adoring the Child, who rests on the ground, while near by the little St. John also kneels. The group is surrounded by five angels, one of whom scatters roses over the Infant, while the others worship him with folded hands.

Among the historical and legendary

subjects illustrative of the life of the Virgin, are those connected with her parents, Joachim and Anna, her Nativity and Presentation in the Temple, and her life there, — her Marriage and all the scenes preceding the Annunciation. Of the latter I have written in connection with the Angel Gabriel. Many of these pictures are very beautiful, and angels are frequently introduced in them.

After the Annunciation follows the Visitation, or the Salutation of Elizabeth. I know of but one fine picture of this scene — by Pinturicchio — in which angels are present at the meeting of the Holy Women. It is a poetic conception, and the humility of the two angels, with downcast eyes and folded hands, gives them the appearance of attendants on the journey of the Virgin, rather than that of witnesses of the Salutation.

The Nativity of Christ, the Adoration

of the Shepherds, and the Adoration of
the Magi — Wise Men — have been represented in a variety of ways, and are
subjects easily distinguished. The first
two are most effective when treated with
perfect simplicity, with no accessories
unsuited to the humble condition of
Joseph and Mary and the Shepherds;
with such scenes the presence of the
angels is in perfect harmony. The Nativity by Albertinelli, in the Uffizi Gallery,
and the Adoration of the Shepherds by
Correggio, in the Dresden gallery, are fine
examples of these subjects.

The Adoration of the Magi, or Kings,
as the legends call them, admits of all
the splendor that an artist desires to
depict. Many pictures of this scene dis-
play magnificent collections of vases,
ewers, and other vessels of gold and silver, while the costumes, jewelled diadems,
and chains of the Kings, are as gorgeous

in texture and color as Veronese, Rubens, Rembrandt, and other artists could make them. Veronese perhaps excelled all others in making his Adoration of the Kings, in the Dresden gallery, an imposing and gorgeous pageant.

Angels are by no means a necessary part of this scene, but are always present in the earliest representations of it. A poetic element is imparted to this picture when the angelic announcement of the birth of Jesus to the Shepherds is introduced in the background; or when the star which directed the Magi in their course appears in the sky, surrounded by angel heads.

In representations of the Flight into Egypt, which Joseph had been directed to make, by an angel in a dream, these heavenly attendants are seen bringing fruits and flowers to the travellers, pitching their tents, leading the ass on which

the Virgin rides, watching over them by
night, and serving them by day.

So in the Repose in Egypt, — one of
the most charming of these kindred
subjects, — the attendant angels are a
delightful feature, and so varied are
their occupations, and so fanciful the
conceits of the painters of this scene,
that many pages might be devoted to a
description of them. For example, Van
Dyck, in his picture in the Ashburton
collection, has represented the Virgin
seated under a spreading tree, holding
the Child, while a number of angels
dance in a round to the music made by
other angels in the clouds above.

Lucas Cranach shows the angels wash-
ing linen; Albert Dürer represents St.
Joseph as shaping a piece of wood with
his axe; some of the many angels present
gather up the chips and put them in
baskets; others dance and frolic merrily

BOUGUEREAU. — THE VIRGIN AND THE ANGELS.

about the group, while still other more serious angels,—probably guardian spirits, —devoutly folding their hands, stand or kneel around the cradle of the Infant Jesus.

Titian, in one of his pictures of this subject, introduced a little angel who waters the ass in a stream. Rembrandt gives his Repose the air of a gipsy camp, which is emphasized by the fact that the only light comes from a lantern hung on a tree. I do not know who painted a Repose that I have seen, to which a very human feeling is imparted by St. Joseph; he is shaking his fist at the ass, which has opened its mouth to bray.

In the almost numberless representations of the Madonna and Child, and of the Holy Family, angels are frequently introduced. These subjects are so easily recognized, and, speaking generally, are so simply treated as to require no comment here.

I have referred to the legend that an angel announced the approach of death to the Virgin Mary, and have explained the difference between the symbolism of this subject, and that of the Annunciation of the birth of Jesus, all of which is made clear by our illustration.

In pictures of the death scene there are always angels present, in greater or lesser numbers. In the representations of the Assumption of the Virgin she is some-times borne upward by angels, and again she ascends without aid. In all cases she is attended by choirs of angels, as in the magnificent Assumption by Titian, which is the pride of the Academy in Venice.

In the purely devotional Assumptions such as that sculptured above the portal of the Cathedral of Florence, — the Santa Maria del Fiore, — the Virgin is within the mandorla, or almond-shaped aureole. She is clothed in white and wears a veil

TITIAN. — THE ASSUMPTION OF THE VIRGIN.

and crown; her hands are joined and she ascends in a glory of light, surrounded by angels. The only special difference in these sculptures is the position of the Virgin, who sometimes sits, and again stands upright, in the mandorla. When the representation corresponds to this, except that the Virgin has no crown, it may more properly be called the Glorification of the Virgin.

Besides the representations of angels who make a part of the devotional and historical scenes in the lives of Christ and the Virgin, of the Evangelists, Apostles, and Fathers of the Church, there are a great number that illustrate the legends of the saints. For example, that of St. Cecilia, whose music charmed even the angelic choirs, so that the angels brought to her the roses of Paradise, is one of the most beautiful.

After the death of St. Catherine of
Alexandria, angels bore her body to the
top of Mount Sinai, as represented in
our illustration by Mücke.

When St. Christina was beaten and
thrown into a dungeon, angels bound up
her wounds, and St. Agatha was comforted by them in her prison.

These are a few examples of the numerous appearances of angels in the legends
of the saints.

Perhaps there are no artistic representations that appeal to a greater number of people, of all possible types, than
do those of angels, in both sculpture and
painting. One reason for this seems to
me to be that angels represent our highest ideal of created beings, — beings that
we can only realize through the power of
imagination, either our own imagination
or that of another. It may be that of a
writer, who, in a vivid word-picture, con-

jures up before us a vision of beings that we have not seen, as do Dante and Milton. Or it may be a sculptor or painter who, rendering his own ideal, helps us to see with his eyes and to accept or reject his work as it appeals to, or repels us.

This recalls the words of Ruskin when he says that the noblest use of imagination is to "enable us to bring sensibly to our sight the things which are recorded as belonging to our future state, or as invisibly surrounding us in this. It is given us, that we may imagine the cloud of witnesses in heaven and earth, and see, as if they were now present, the souls of the righteous waiting for us; that we may conceive the great army of the inhabitants of heaven, and discover among them those whom we most desire to be with forever; that we may be able to vision forth the ministry of angels beside us, and see the chariots of fire on the mountains that gird

us round; but, above all, to call up the
scenes and. facts in which we are commanded to believe, and be present, as if
in the body, at every recorded event of
the history of the Redeemer."

With such a thought in mind, it is well
worth while to study the various types of
angels which are a rich portion of the
legacies of the artists to the world. It
is surely right to attempt to imagine
the glories of a sphere beyond this,—
a heaven of purity and glory. One of
the most powerful aids to this imagination is the contemplation of religious
pictures, especially those that were executed with such reverence and sincerity
as make them appear to reproduce actual
scenes, and, for the time, carry us out of
ourselves and into the imaginary earth
and heaven of the master whose works
we study.

Thus we may leave this brief review of

the subject of Angels in Art, feeling that its further development by each reader for himself is a pursuit in harmony with St. Paul's admonition: " Whatsoever things are pure, whatsoever things are lovely, whatsoever things are of good report; if there be any virtue, and if there be any praise, think on these things."

THE END.

INDEX.

www.ingramcontent.com/pod-product-compliance
Lightning Source LLC
Chambersburg PA
CBHW030356270326
41926CB00009B/1132